TRUTH

THE CHURCH AT ANTIOCH

FIRST-CENTURY LESSONS FOR CHURCH LIFE TODAY

William Nelson

DayOne

ISBN 978-1-84625-600-4

British Library Cataloguing in Publication Data available

Published by Day One Publications
Ryelands Road, Leominster, HR6 8NZ
Telephone 01568 613 740 FAX 01568 611 473
email—sales@dayone.co.uk
web site—www.dayone.co.uk

Cover design by Kathryn Chedgzoy
Printed by TJ International

Dedicated to my four adult children
Julie, Mandy, Paul and Hannah.
For their love and grace

Acknowledgements

I would like to express my thanks to all at Day One, without whom this book would not have come into being, and to Suzanne Mitchell for her work editing the text. I also thank my wife, Joan, for her faithful encouragement.

Contents

Time-travelling

In this book I invite you to travel back in time with me, back to the year AD 45. The television character Dr Who has a Tardis in which to travel through time, but we will need only our imaginations to take us to our intended destination. I would like you to travel with me to a city called Antioch.

Antioch was the third-largest city in the Roman Empire, and capital of the province of Syria. The city was built beside the river Orontes and boasted a fine seaport, Seleucia Pieria. As well as being an important trade and commercial centre, it was also renowned for its culture. However, our visit to Antioch is not in order to consider its commercial importance, nor to view its architectural treasures or experience its artistic culture; rather, it is to visit the church that has been founded there.

This church has a large congregation (Acts 11:21b, 24b), and because many Greeks had responded to the message of Jesus Christ and come to trust in Him for salvation, it qualifies for the title of the first Gentile church (11:20–21). I am sure you will have heard of the person who is the elder, or pastor, of this fellowship of believers: it is none other than Barnabas (11:22). The associate minister, brought in by Barnabas to be his assistant, is none other than Saul, who became better known as Paul, the first Christian missionary (11:25). Perhaps details like these will help you understand why we would wish to visit this church in Antioch.

If we have any difficulty in locating the church, I have a sneaking suspicion that, if we were to ask any inhabitant of the city for directions, he or she would be able to point us in the right direction. I make this claim because it was at Antioch that the followers of Jesus were first given the pseudonym 'Christians' (11:26b)—an indicator, I sense, of the influence the church had on the community, as well as its fame. As we make our way through the streets of Antioch, perhaps I ought to tell you a little more about this fledgling church we are about to visit.

The first mention of Antioch in the New Testament comes when there is a dispute regarding the daily distribution of food to widows. The church was at that time still predominantly Jewish in nature, and still centred in Jerusalem. However, in this instance Grecian Jews complained that their widows were being overlooked and that preference was being given to the Hebraic Jews' dependants (Acts 6:1). The solution to this local difficulty, as you perhaps know, was to appoint seven men from among the congregation who were full of the Holy Spirit and wisdom, and give to them the responsibility of distributing the daily rations (6:3). Of these seven men, Stephen and Philip are the best known, but we read from the list that one of these deacons, Nicolas, was from Antioch (6:5). Nicolas was a Greek who had evidently converted to Judaism and had subsequently accepted Jesus as his Saviour. From this information we may deduce that there was a strong and active, if small, Jewish Christian community in Antioch, of which Nicolas was a respected member, even being accepted in the fellowship at Jerusalem. The city of Antioch is thus brought to our attention by this mention of Nicolas' appointment as a deacon.

Following the martyrdom of Stephen, the church in Jerusalem suffered harsh, cruel persecution, and all the Christians, except the apostles, were forced to flee for safety. Initially, they were mainly scattered throughout Judea and Samaria (8:1), but eventually they spread out as far as Phoenicia, Cyprus and Antioch (11:19). To begin with, these fleeing Christians spoke only to the Jews, no doubt seeking to persuade them that Jesus was their Messiah. However, at length, some men from Cyprus and Cyrene began to preach the good news of the Lord Jesus to the Gentiles of Antioch (11:19–20), with amazing results: many people responded to their message (11:21). The church began to increase in numbers, and news of this growth reached the mother church in Jerusalem. We can but conjecture as to what the reaction to this news was, but we know that it caused the elders to send Barnabas up to Antioch to investigate the credibility of this revival (11:22).

If the pillars of the church in Jerusalem had any reservations or fears with regard to this matter, the news reports from Barnabas would soon have allayed their concerns. At Antioch Barnabas found evidence of the grace of God at work, which gladdened his heart—so much so that he stayed in that city and ministered to the members of that young church, to nurture and encourage them in their new-found faith (11:23). Barnabas, we are informed, was a 'good man, full of the Holy Spirit' (11:24), and as a result of his ministry, the church expanded further—to the extent that Barnabas felt compelled to seek assistance in his task of teaching and leading this church. This is where the apostle Paul (still known as Saul at this point) is drawn into the situation. Barnabas, who at one time was a mentor or sponsor of Paul (9:26–29), went to Tarsus, Paul's home city, and brought him to Antioch to share in the ministry there. It was a successful ministry; for a year they taught many who were hungry to learn and increase their knowledge of God (11:25–26).

This must have been an exciting time—not only for the church, growing in the knowledge of the Lord and seeing an increase in membership, but also for the community. The ripples of what was happening in that church must have spread out to touch the citizens of the city, causing them to coin the name 'Christians' to describe these exuberant believers (11:26b).

There must have been a great outreach across the city, with many more coming to faith. Archaeological excavations on the site of the old city have discovered ruins of at least twenty churches dating from the first century. However, on the occasion of this visit of ours to Antioch, that growth has not yet taken place and there is perhaps just one meeting place. So let us weave our way through the streets and hesitantly, yet with great anticipation, join these young Christians at worship. And let us see what we can learn from this Gentile church, the forerunner of many more to come. Let us try to discover what it was that enabled this church to be fruitful and effective for the Lord. Let us travel back in time.

Chapter 1

A well-led church

In the church at Antioch there were prophets and teachers ... (Acts 13:1)

As we begin to examine the characteristics of the church at Antioch, it is important to say that we are not considering them in any order of importance. Our observations are made randomly, for all the traits are in some way only the parts of a whole.

Godly leaders in Antioch

One of the distinctive marks of a church which will grow and be effective is that it is well led by godly pastors and elders. When I was seeking to encourage you to accompany me on this visit to this church, I told you that Barnabas and Paul (then called Saul) were deeply involved in the teaching and leadership of the congregation, Barnabas having been sent by the church at Jerusalem to investigate the veracity of the news of the emerging church at Antioch (Acts 11:22). Initially, it seems that Barnabas assumed a leadership role, possibly with sole responsibility for the church's programme (11:22–23). However, it must have become evident to him that the responsibility for the ongoing strengthening, encouragement and growth was beyond the capabilities of one person. So, perhaps with great discernment, insight and humility, he sought out an assistant. You will recall that Barnabas travelled to Tarsus and persuaded Paul to become involved in the ministry of this growing fellowship (11:25–26). So at this point we see that the leadership team consisted of at least two people. There was a shared leadership.

However, under these two godly men the church had continued to expand and grow, and consequently it must have become necessary to increase the leadership team. Further teachers and prophets were appointed, and when we read about the church in Acts 13 we discover that this team now totalled five: Barnabas and Paul were still involved, but to them had been added Simeon, Manaen and Lucius (13:1). So here we discover a church with a team ministry of at least five elders. The leadership is plural; it is not the domain of just one person.

However, important as it is that the leadership of the church is in the control not of a single person but of a team, it is essential that the team is constituted of *godly* men—men of *God*. We recall that when the disciples, under Peter's leading, were seeking to replace Judas, the qualifications included having been with the company since the baptism of Jesus through to His ascension—that is, someone who knew Christ, a godly man. Matthias, of course, fulfilled this requirement (Acts 1:12–26).

Barnabas' credentials in this area are noted quite clearly, as he is described as a man 'full of the Holy Spirit and faith' (11:24). Over and above this, the Greek root word of his name, Barnabas, which means 'Son of Encouragement' (4:36), is *paraklesis*, a word also used in respect of the Holy Spirit. You may have noted that Barnabas was not his birth name: this was Joseph. A Levite from Cyprus, he obviously acquired the name Barnabas as a pseudonym because of his character and his godliness.

Who would doubt the testimonial of Paul in this respect? Apart from the evidence of his subsequent life and ministry, we read that, after his meeting with Jesus on the way to Damascus, he had to await the arrival of Ananias. And the purpose of Ananias' visit? To pray that Paul would recover his sight and be filled with the Holy Spirit (9:17)—the latter being a necessity for a man of God. Paul himself, when writing to the church at Rome, is emphatic as he tells them that without the Holy Spirit one does not belong to Christ. The Spirit is the mark, the sign, of our belonging to Christ (Rom. 8:9) and also the source of the Christian servant's power for effective ministry (Acts 1:8). Indeed, we note that when Barnabas and Paul embarked on their first missionary journey, it was at the instigation of the Holy Spirit (Acts 13:4).

What of the three other members of the ministry team: Simeon, Lucius and Manaen? Well, we do know that it was when they were worshipping, fasting and praying together with Barnabas and Paul that the Holy Spirit spoke to them (13:2). Surely these evidences are sufficient to confirm the godliness of these three leaders: worshipping, fasting and prayerful; spoken to by, and obedient to, the Holy Spirit; and being associated with Barnabas and Paul. What better references could one require?

We need to study further this matter of godly leadership as it is very significant for the nurturing and strengthening of a healthy church. Let us begin by looking at some negatives, considering God's displeasure with ungodly leadership. To do this we will turn to the Old Testament and some words of condemnation uttered by the prophet Ezekiel.

Biblical descriptions of ungodly leadership

In the opening words of Ezekiel 34 we are informed that the 'shepherds of Israel'—obviously those with a responsibility to govern the people aright—were primarily interested in themselves. Their minds were dominated by self-concern (34:2). Along with self-concern goes self-preservation; or, as the prophet says, they fed themselves on the best food, curds and choice cuts of meat, and grandly clothed themselves in wool (v. 3). Verses 2 and 3 end with the same accusation about their approach to the flock: they did not care for the sheep!

This is, of course, figurative language, as the true concern was the people of Israel, not sheep. The next verse (v. 4) gives us further details with regard to their lack of care, enumerating examples of the attention the leaders had failed to offer. The shepherds had ignored and failed to extend any support to the weak, the sick and the injured. Those who were ill—physically, emotionally, spiritually—had been deserted, left, without any ministry or counsel, to continue in their pain. And those who had strayed or become lost had been ignored, allowed to wander away. They had not been recalled or even searched for.

As well as this laxity in oversight, we note that the shepherds had exercised their authority in a brutal and harsh manner (v. 4). We can describe this leadership (which is really a lack of leadership) that is condemned as truly worthless and contemptible; the resultant chaos was to be expected. What the prophet describes is the definition of ungodly ministry (vv. 5–6). I am sure that the godly ministry at Antioch was a total contrast to what we have just considered.

If we are to learn from these verses the attributes of godly leadership, we will have to ponder the opposite of these shepherds' behaviour. So, taking that approach, what type of person will a godly leader be?

Biblical descriptions of godly leadership

CARE AND COMPASSION

It would seem obvious that the first attribute of a godly leader should be a heartfelt care and concern for the well-being of the flock. This attitude is, of course, completely in line with Jesus' ministry; we read on several occasions that, as He looked out over the crowds, or when He was in individual contact with someone, He had compassion on them (e.g. Matt. 9:36; Luke 15:20). Although the word 'love' is not mentioned in these verses—nor in Paul's instructions to Timothy (1 Tim. 3:2–7) or in the words of Peter (1 Peter 5:2–3), which we will look at below—it is nevertheless surely an unspoken requirement. It is impossible to feel any care, concern or compassion without love.

One of the best illustrations of the requirement for love and care in the life of a pastor is when Jesus reinstated Peter and commissioned him for ministry after Jesus' crucifixion and resurrection (John 21:15–17). The disciples had gone fishing when Jesus appeared on the lakeside, and eventually they dined together. As the alfresco meal came to an end, Jesus spoke specifically to Simon Peter. Jesus' initial appeal to Peter was the thrice-pressed question, 'Do you love me?' Peter replied each time in the affirmative, but as well as this emphasis Jesus placed on love He appealed to Peter to 'feed my lambs', 'take care of my sheep' and 'feed the sheep'—in other words, Peter must care for the flock. Jesus was initiating Peter into the pastor's role and in so doing stressed that the important characteristic of such service is care undergirded by love. No wonder that, as we will see later, Peter was able to write to the elders of the churches in Asia Minor and offer them clear instructions concerning the role of a pastor (1 Peter 5:2–3); it was Jesus' expectation of him.

When we read advertisements setting forth attributes for a required pastor, how often do we read that the basic requirement is love revealed in compassion? 'Caring' is an overriding word, but for it to have any meaning there must be some practical outworking. Staying with what we have read already in Ezekiel, we see that care should reveal itself in the feeding and nurturing of the flock. Although we would spiritualize this point—that is, seeing the pastor's main function as teaching from the Scriptures and praying for the people under his care, which is of course correct—we know also, from the difficulty faced by the young church at Jerusalem regarding the position of the widows, that providing physical sustenance for the poor, doing something practical, should be part of the church's programme too (Acts 6:1–7). Yes, in Jerusalem the elders had to be freed to 'give attention to prayer and the ministry of the word', but I am sure that in their hearts they carried a burden for the poor, even though the practicalities were undertaken by others.

THE EXAMPLE OF THE SERVANT OF THE LORD

We also learn from the negatives in Ezekiel that a pastor should be someone who will seek to encourage believers, heal the hurting, reclaim the straying and seek the lost. The words of Isaiah regarding the Servant of the Lord are relevant in this respect too. Although we associate the words with Jesus, they also have some relevance for any pastor:

A bruised reed he will not break,
and a smouldering wick he will not snuff out.
(Isa. 42:3)

The Spirit of the Sovereign LORD is on me,
because the LORD has anointed me
to preach good news to the poor.
He has sent me to bind up the broken-hearted,
to proclaim freedom for the captives
and release from darkness for the prisoners,
to proclaim the year of the LORD's favour
and the day of vengeance of our God,
to comfort all who mourn,
and provide for those who grieve in Zion.
(Isa. 61:1–3a)

Jesus took these words as referring to Himself when He read them in the synagogue at Nazareth (Luke 4:16–19).

PETER'S INSTRUCTIONS IN 1 PETER 5:2–4

How often it is that our expectations of a pastor are linked with what we consider he ought to *do*, when really our assumptions should be based around what he *is*—someone who will be involved in the deepest concerns of the flock. The apostle Peter, when writing to the churches in the region of modern-day Turkey, demonstrates this approach (1 Peter 5:2–4). His opening emphasis in these verses is that elders are principally shepherds who must care for their flocks. Although they are given responsibility as overseers, this ministry must be exercised in the spirit of servanthood. Be 'eager to serve', exhorts Peter. Again we are conscious, as we would expect, that Jesus is the prime example in this area: 'For even the Son of

Man did not come to be served, but to serve, and to give his life as a ransom for many' (Mark 10:45).

Peter adds that the pastoral ministry is to be exercised willingly (v. 2), not reluctantly; not because they must, not because there is no one else for the task or because someone thinks they should 'give it a try'. No, a willingness for the task is required, together with a consciousness that one is called by God, that one is serving in accord with God's will. It should not be for monetary gain, either. In other words, there are hints here of self-denial, which are further emphasized by Peter's appeal for humility: 'not lording it over those entrusted to you' (v. 3). They should seek not to please men but God, who will utter any words of commendation and award the crown of glory (v. 4). The apostle Paul wrote at the close of his ministry of having given himself totally to the call he had received from the Lord, of having 'fought the good fight' and having 'finished the race', and of awaiting the 'crown of righteousness' from the 'righteous Judge' (2 Tim. 4:6–8). Paul's life, as well as his self-penned epitaph, is a clear example of the loving, caring, dedicated service of a servant-pastor under the Chief Shepherd.

PAUL'S EXAMPLE AND TEACHING

Earlier, when writing to the churches of Galatia, Paul wrote that his object in ministry was not to please men, but God (Gal. 1:10), and surely this should be the aim and consequently the mark of godly leaders—not necessarily antagonizing people, but 'speaking the truth in love' (Eph. 4:15). After all, we have just been considering how a pastor should care for and have compassion on his flock, and such a one would not deliberately cause strife; yet primarily it is God whom he serves and seeks to please.

When considering Paul's attitude and manner in the fulfilment of his ministry, we cannot but remind ourselves of the words he wrote to the church in Corinth which reveal the depth of his concern for those to whom he was ministering. After listing all the troubles and difficulties he had faced in the service of the Lord—beatings, dangers, hunger, cold, and so on—he adds, 'Besides everything else, I face daily the pressure of my concern for all the churches' (2 Cor. 11:28).

As we have turned to the life and ministry of Paul for examples of godly leadership, it is appropriate that we turn now to some of Paul's teaching on the subject (1 Tim. 3:2–7). Paul, like Peter, was concerned with the character and personality of an overseer. While he says that an overseer must be able to teach (v. 2), which one would deem essential together with prayerfulness, it does seem that at this point it is character with which Paul is concerned (we shall examine preaching, teaching and praying in detail in later chapters). So what does Paul say?

Look at the detailed and comprehensive list of qualifications. According to Paul, an overseer should be:

- above reproach
- the husband of one wife (controversial for more than one reason)
- temperate
- self-controlled
- respectable
- hospitable
- (able to teach)
- sober
- gentle
- peaceable
- generous
- deserving respect (even that of his own children)
- not a recent convert
- with a good reputation among outsiders.

As we consider these attributes of godly leadership, it is little wonder that Paul could write, as he considered the ministry, 'And who is equal to such a task?' (2 Cor. 2:16). How logical too that, as he responds to his own rhetorical question, he should state, 'our competence comes from God' (3:5).

ENCOURAGING FUTURE LEADERS

It seems likely that Paul looked for a further attribute in the lives of pastors and leaders. We discover this almost hidden among some words of encouragement that he wrote to Timothy: 'Be strong in the grace that is in Christ Jesus,' he writes (2 Tim. 2:1); then he continues, saying that he expects Timothy to 'entrust [Paul's teaching] to reliable men who will also be qualified to teach others' (2:2). Paul seems to expect Timothy to be able to discern possible future leaders and to train them for ministry in the years ahead. The task of looking out for further leaders in this way does have biblical warrant. From our perspective, it is quite evident from reading Paul's letters to Timothy, and other letters too, that Paul had chosen and groomed Timothy for future leadership. From the context of the letters it is clear that, initially at least, this leadership was carried out at Ephesus (1 Tim. 1:3). We could say also that Titus had been chosen and trained for leadership too, in his case in Crete (Titus 1:5). What Paul had done in preparing Timothy (and Titus) for ministry he expected to be continued as part of Timothy's ministry.

We can find further examples of this principle in the Old Testament—with Moses, no less. Alongside Moses' mission to bring the people of Israel out of Egypt and into Canaan was the parallel task of training a successor. This was to be Joshua son of Nun, who as Moses' servant had accompanied him up Mount Sinai (Exod. 24:13). Looking to the future, Moses had asked the Lord to appoint his successor (Num. 27:15–17). The Lord's response was the election of Joshua (Num. 27:18–21). In his farewell address to the people of Israel, Moses reminded them that Joshua was his chosen successor, and as part of the discourse singled him out and commissioned him for the final part of the journey to and settlement in the Promised Land (Deut. 1:38; 31:7–8). God Himself endorsed Joshua's appointment after Moses' death (Josh. 1:1–9), the people having already accepted him (Deut. 34:9). We could also note that in some way Eli prepared Samuel to be his successor; and David (although it caused a family upset) chose Solomon as the future king of Israel.

The ultimate example of choosing and preparing others for future ministry is Jesus Himself. He trained his disciples to carry forth the Good News to future generations, to be His witnesses (Matt. 28:19–20; Acts 1:8). In a sense, this is the process Paul had carried on when he called Timothy to do the same in 2 Timothy 2:2. Indeed, such preparation for the future has continued down the centuries until today, and needs to continue. It is essential that leaders should be able to discern potential successors.

Because the emphases in the passages we have considered are directed to elders and pastors, we have concentrated our thoughts in that direction. However, although it is important to consider biblical guidelines when making appointments to the overall leadership, it would be remiss of us if we did not take into account consideration of these characteristics when appointing leaders to other areas of ministry. There is a danger of being lax in the appointment of leaders to other positions—that is, there is often a lack of prayer and consideration of spiritual graces and gifts. Before the appointment of overall leaders there is often great agonizing in prayer; should the same diligence not be shown with selections to other positions? Surely it is in error if we appoint someone to a position of responsibility without serious prayer and consideration. Sadly, this often happens. The discussion points at the end of this chapter can be applied to all positions of leadership.

THE ROLE OF THE HOLY SPIRIT

The characteristics we have looked at as qualification for positions of leadership can be summed up in two words: Holy Spirit. While we must remember that it is the qualifications themselves to which we must pay heed when considering how a church can be well led, these are of course evidence of the Holy Spirit's presence and call. Remember that the first pastor of the church we are visiting at Antioch, Barnabas, 'was a good man, full of the Holy Spirit and faith' (Acts 11:24). When Zechariah was told by the angel of the Lord that his wife Elizabeth was to give birth to a son who would be the Lord's messenger, the angel said that the child 'will be filled with the Holy Spirit even from birth' (Luke 1:15). Before the disciples could be involved in ministry, particularly their early evangelistic proclamations, they first had to wait to receive the Holy Spirit, who duly arrived at Pentecost (Acts 1:8; 2:4). The seven deacons appointed to wait at tables, and especially Stephen, one of their number, were said to be 'full of the Spirit', 'full of faith and of the Holy Spirit' (Acts 6:3, 5). Before he began the ministry to which the Lord was calling him, the apostle Paul too, immediately after his confrontation with Jesus outside Damascus, was visited by Ananias, 'to see again and be filled with the Holy Spirit' (Acts 9:17). And we remind ourselves that our Lord Jesus was assured of the Holy Spirit's presence, by the descent of the dove and the word of God, as He commenced His ministry (Matt. 3:16; Mark 1:10; Luke 3:22).

In future chapters we will consider further the influence of and dependence on the Holy Spirit, but for now we should note the importance of the fruit of the Spirit in the lives of leaders; 'if I ... have not love, I am nothing ... I gain nothing' (1 Cor. 13:2–3).

Now, as we approach the church at Antioch, we remind ourselves that love undergirds all the qualities and gifts required for good leadership. It does not replace them or negate them, which is a trap into which those responsible for the appointment of leaders sometimes fall. Yes, love is essential, but the requirements listed by Peter and Paul, and a willingness to be a servant, are also necessary. We noted at the beginning of this chapter that the church at Antioch was a well-led church, with godly leadership, and it should be our constant prayer that God would raise up godly leaders for today's churches. Hopefully we may learn something from the church at Antioch to guide us in this vitally important area of the church's life. It is possible that the apostle Paul, during the time he spent with the leadership team in Antioch, learnt some lessons about leadership, and when he penned his instructions on the subject in his letters, particularly those addressed to Timothy and Titus, these were based on experience and practice, not on theory. If so, Paul had observed the God-given way to good, godly leadership and was passing it on. If Paul could so learn, surely we can too; indeed, we must do so.

To think about

» List all the leadership roles in your church.

» How much prayerful consideration and regard for the biblical qualifications we have examined in this chapter was given to the appointments of those in each role you have listed? Grade each appointment from 1 (none) to 5 (a lot). How should what we have considered in this chapter affect future decisions?

» If there is no person 'suitably qualified' to fulfil a particular leadership role, how much consideration would your fellowship give to not making an appointment? Think about positions on your church committee, roles within children's work, and so on. Would you simply resort to choosing someone who was available?

» How serious are you in your fellowship with regard to the appointment of people not only to leadership roles, but also for practical tasks? (Remember the appointment of the deacons in Acts 6:1–7.)

» How might any change in approach in this respect affect the overall approach

Chapter 2

A well-fed church

In the church at Antioch there were prophets and teachers ... (Acts 13:1)

As we walk through the streets of Antioch towards the church which meets in that city, you may find that, having received my assurance that it is a well-led church, your mind has strayed to ponder what the sermon or the teaching will be like. Well, I promise you that you will discover that this church is not only well led, but it is also well fed! It is well taught. This matter, of course, goes together with the church being well led: one would expect godly instruction to be a corollary of godly leadership. No doubt you are saying to yourself, 'If Paul and Barnabas are part of the leadership team, the teaching should be of prime quality!' We would assume that such a fellowship will be receiving clear instruction and tuition in the tenets of the faith and its outworking in life; that it is soundly taught regarding Christian belief and behaviour.

I believe that we receive clear confirmation of these expectations when we turn again to the beginning of Acts 13. There the five members of the leadership team are described as 'prophets' and 'teachers' (v. 1). Surely there are deep implications of the fact that they are recognized in the Word of God as teachers!

The importance of knowing the Word of God in the Old Testament

In the Scriptures, great importance is attached to the people of God being well versed in the Word of God. Implicit in the Lord's condemnation of the shepherds of Israel in the prophecy of Ezekiel, which we examined in our previous chapter, is the fact that they fed themselves but did not feed the flock with the 'living and enduring word of God' (1 Peter 1:23). The importance of the Word of God for the people of God is written indelibly in their history. From the very beginning we read of how essential it was for the people of Israel to be aware of the Lord's Word and to be obedient to it.

For example, as Moses comes towards the close of his last will and testament, as recorded in Deuteronomy, we discover that he has written down the law—the word from God delivered at Mount Sinai. He passed this scroll to the priests and the sons of Levi for safe-keeping. He then commanded that every seven years, when the people assembled for the cancellation of debts during the Feast of Tabernacles, the law should be read in the hearing of all the people: men, women, children and foreigners among them. The purpose? That they might learn to fear the Lord and follow carefully all the words of the law (Deut. 31:9–13).

Two further examples from the Old Testament demonstrate this importance of the Word of God. First we go to the days of one of the kings, King Josiah. He was a godly king. While repairs to the temple were taking place under Hilkiah the high priest, the Book of the Law was discovered among the rubble and rubbish that had accumulated due to previous neglect. The impressed yet humbled Josiah ordered the Book of the Covenant to be read in the presence of the people of Jerusalem, after which he and all the people, from the least to the greatest, pledged themselves to the covenant. This resulted in revival and a cleansing of the ungodly, pagan objects and worship that had overrun the land (2 Kings 22:1–23:3).

In a later period in the history of Israel, when the people had returned from exile in Babylon and had started to resettle the land, we find the prophet and priest Ezra reading from the book of the Law of Moses. Standing on a raised platform Ezra read all morning, and as he read the Levites instructed the people so that they could understand what was being read. An exposition was given simultaneously to the reading. The result was a spontaneous outburst of worship and praise to God—in other words, revival (Neh. 8:1–8).

The importance of knowing the Word of God in the New Testament

As we move into the New Testament, we read that the synagogue and its weekly instruction in the Word of God was an integral part of Jewish life in which Jesus Himself participated. We have records of His attendance at the synagogue (Luke 4:15) and of His preaching there too (Luke 4:21; Matt. 4:23; 9:35; 13:54, etc.).

Because of what we know about Barnabas and Paul from the general picture we have of their lives, the assumption is that their preaching would have been efficacious and helpful. This premise is strengthened by our knowledge of their religious background, which involved regular instruction in the Old Testament Scriptures. Being taught comprehensively and regularly from the Scriptures was deeply ingrained in their lives, and they would naturally have continued in that godly activity in their own ministry. We recall that Paul could even have been rather boastful of his religious education; he told the churches in Galatia that he 'was advancing in Judaism beyond many Jews of my own age and was extremely jealous for the traditions of the fathers' (Gal. 1:14). He was top of the class! A student at Jerusalem University, 'Under Gamaliel I was thoroughly trained in the law of our fathers' (Acts 22:3).

Surely nothing can give greater emphasis to the importance of the Scriptures than the fact that, when Jesus came to dwell on the earth, He was called 'the Word'—the living embodiment of the written and spoken word of God. He was the Word made flesh (John 1:1, 14). The opening verses of the Epistle to the Hebrews provide further confirmation that God was speaking to His world through His Son: 'In the past God spoke to our forefathers through the prophets ... but in these last days he has spoken to us by his Son' (Heb. 1:1–2). Not only was Jesus the living message from God, but we find that, as the living Word, Jesus also spoke the Word. He taught His disciples! The clearest example of this is the Sermon on the Mount (Matt. 5–7). Jesus taught the crowds, not just in the synagogue but in the open air, often beside the lake (Mark 2:13, etc.). Even His opponents recognized that He taught the Word of God, and the way of God, the truth (Luke 20:21). Jesus' expectation of His disciples was that they would continue to teach the message of God (be His witnesses, Acts 1:8); though His teaching of them may initially have been limited by their lack of understanding, when the time came for deeper insight the Holy Spirit would guide them into all truth (John 16:12–13). In addition, during His conversation with Peter at the lakeside, after His resurrection, Jesus was more specific and instructed Peter to 'Feed my lambs', 'Take care of my sheep' (John 21:15–17).

Teaching in the church

In the previous chapter we made passing mention of Paul's instruction that elders should be able to teach (1 Tim. 3:2; see also 2 Tim. 2:2; 24). This is clearly a requirement of a pastor or elder. 'Timothy,' says Paul, 'when you appoint elders, as well as them being people who care, they must be able teachers.' They must be men who could pass on the teaching they had heard from Timothy, who in turn had received it from Paul; they needed to be reliable men.

At this point it is helpful to recall Timothy's own background in the faith. We note that Timothy was encouraged to continue in what he had learnt (2 Tim. 3:14–15). Paul reminds him of those who had been his teachers (they were probably his mother and grandmother), and prompts him to remember that it was this teaching which made him wise (we will return to this passage again shortly).

The early days of the church at Antioch were founded on the instruction of devoted and gifted teaching. We know that Barnabas and Paul, for a whole year, taught great numbers; the congregation grew and its fame spread (Acts 11:26).

The serious consequences of a lack of Bible teaching

Before we consider the benefits of solid biblical teaching, let us first turn our thoughts to the opposite scenario: the consequences of a lack of detailed instruction eagerly assimilated.

The Bible often uses food as a metaphor for teaching. Paul is one of the apostles who uses food in this way. Coupled with this analogy is that of infancy and maturity, stagnation and growth, spirituality and worldliness. As he writes to the Corinthian Christians Paul expresses disappointment because their spiritual growth is limited: they are the equivalent of infants (1 Cor. 3:1–3). He is having to feed them on milk, as they are not yet ready for solid food. They have not yet grasped even the elementary spiritual truths and are behaving in worldly ways—jealousy and quarrelling, divisions, factions and partisanship—with dire consequences for the health of the church and their personal spiritual growth. He calls them 'worldly—mere infants'. In the remainder of his letter Paul has to correct them regarding immorality, a lack of discretion with regard to food offered to idols, inappropriate behaviour at the Lord's Supper, a superior attitude with regard to spiritual gifts, and a lack of love.

The writer of the Epistle to the Hebrews addresses a similar problem, telling his readers they are slow to learn (Heb. 5:12–13). As yet they are not qualified to be teachers and are in need of tutoring in the basic elements of the faith 'all over again'! He uses the same analogy as Paul, informing them that they are still infants in the faith, still needing milk and not yet weaned. But how does this condition manifest itself in their lives? Initially we see that there is something lacking in their Christian experience: a lack of growth and spiritual understanding; and as we have already mentioned, they are incapable of being teachers, still needing to be taught themselves. A further lack is in the gift of discernment: they are unable to distinguish between good and evil (5:14). They also lack maturity. Their faith and understanding have not been stretched; there is a need for the repetition of the basic elements of the faith (6:1–2). By analogy we also discover that they are unfruitful. This should be obvious, of course: fruitfulness flows from abiding in Christ and obedience to His commands (John 15:1–5; Heb. 6:7–8). Limited understanding would not be very helpful in this respect. And, finally, we notice that there is a possibility of their falling away, which if not addressed will have eternal consequences (6:4–6).

From these two passages, then, we note that the lack of teaching has dire consequences for the Christian and for the Christian church. This might prompt us to analyse the current state of the Christian church, and in particular consider the relationship between its present ineffectualness and weakness, and the lack of biblical teaching.

The serious consequences of a lack of application of Bible teaching

While there is clearly danger in the lack of instruction, there is also danger in the reluctance on the part of some Christians to apply themselves to hearing or reading gospel teaching. In this respect we must remind ourselves of a situation which benefited greatly from sound teaching.

TEACHING = GROWTH?

Let's go back in time to recall the church in its early days in Jerusalem shortly after Pentecost. As a result of Simon Peter's Pentecost Day sermon, 'about three thousand were added to their number' (Acts 2:41). That's a lot of people! We are told that all these people were baptized. The next piece of information we are given regarding this group—the crucial data in respect of our current study of this infant church—was that they 'devoted themselves to the apostles' teaching' (Acts 2:42). This suggests they were eager to know more of the gospel and anxious to grow in discipleship. We are told in that verse of other evidences of their Christian commitment, but for now we allow this one fact to sink into our understanding: they devoted themselves to the apostles' teaching. And, as we read further about this emergent Christian fellowship, we are told that the Lord continued to add to their number, on a daily basis (2:47). Was this growth, then, a consequence of the church's commitment to Jesus, and in particular to His Word? Or was the increase simply a coincidence? You will recall that this outcome is similar to that which followed the teaching of Paul and Barnabas during their early days in Antioch (Acts 11:25–26). Sound teaching, and its acceptance and application among the congregation, produced Christian growth. There was quality and quantity.

At this point, we may be in danger of believing that the way for the church to grow numerically—or spiritually—is for it to possess consistent biblical teachers: fine expositors and faithful instructors of Bible truth. This is certainly true in one respect (indeed, it is the basis of our thesis!). However, experience tells us to proceed with caution as there is clear evidence that such an outcome is not always the case. There are at least two reasons why we should not be too dogmatic.

The first is that, as well as possessing gifted teachers, the church, as has already been implied, must also consist of those who are 'devoted ... to the apostles' teaching'. It is not just the gifted teaching or attendance at a well-fed, well-taught church that creates any growth; the Word has to dwell richly within its hearers (Col. 3:16). There must be Word-hungry Christians.

Secondly, we must recognize that Word = growth is not a magic formula, because there are some fellowships where the Word is preached faithfully and is eagerly heard and applied, yet, sadly, growth is withheld. There are some situations where, in spite of faithful preaching, prayer and outreach, there is no numerical growth; indeed, the opposite seems to apply.

The implications of the examples we noted in the letters to Corinth and the Hebrews is not that they had not heard sound teaching, but that they had not received it. The Christians to whom those letters were addressed were content to stay in the elementary class—to stay imbibing milk rather than digesting meat—and consequently they lacked Christian maturity. They were an example of the rocky ground in Jesus' parable of the sower. Deprived of nourishment, the seed sown on this ground withered; it was the seed that fell on good soil that stood for 'those with a noble and good heart, who hear the word, retain it, and by persevering produce a crop' (Luke 8:15; see 8:1–15). As Paul wrote to the church at Philippi, 'Whatever you have learned or received or heard from me, or seen in me—put it into practice' (Phil. 4:9).

We can be assured, then, that the church in Antioch was not only fed well by gifted teachers (e.g. Barnabas and Paul), but that the teaching was received by devoted hearers who yearned to apply what they heard. There was a desire for the Word of God; a longing to know and understand its meaning. It is not just the hearing of the Word that brings this benefit, but the doing of it also. James wrote, 'Do not merely listen to the word and so deceive yourselves. Do what it says' (James 1:22). He was but quoting from the words of his half-brother, none other than Jesus Himself: 'Blessed … are those who hear the word of God and obey it' (Luke 11:28); 'My mother and brothers are those who hear God's word and put it into practice' (Luke 8:21).

Perhaps you feel that the evidence for the Antioch Christians' eagerness for the Word of God is circumstantial; the example of the approach of the Christians at Berea is, however, quite explicit: 'The Bereans were of more noble character than the Thessalonians, for they received the message with great eagerness and examined the Scriptures every day' (Acts 17:11).

Now we must note the benefits which arise from the teaching and application of the Scriptures.

The benefits of the teaching and application of the Scriptures

TELLING FUTURE GENERATIONS

The apostle Paul left his protégé, the young man Timothy, in charge of the church at Ephesus. Writing to him in 2 Timothy, Paul stressed the importance of knowledge of the Word of God for Timothy's spiritual well-being. Timothy, we learn, although still a young man, had been familiar with the Scriptures since he was a child (2 Tim. 3:15)—the inference being that he became acquainted with the Word of God in his home through the influence of his mother and grandmother (1:5). That should cause us to consider the importance of Bible teaching for children, that they may grow up with a sound biblical knowledge. It is a family responsibility.

This is, of course, an Old Testament principle laid down by Moses in his final instructions to the people of Israel. Moses is reminding the people about the importance of the commandments, the decrees and statutes of the Lord, and the necessity of obedience to them. But these injunctions were not given simply for the benefit of one generation; they are for all time. Therefore it is important that future generations are aware that these commands are an essential part of their relationship with God. So what does Moses command? 'Teach them to your children and to their children after them' (Deut. 4:9). This emphasis of passing on the message to grandchildren as well as children, with its implication that all future generations are included, was stressed by God Himself as He commanded Moses to return to Pharaoh before the plague of locusts: '... tell your children and your grandchildren ...' (Exod. 10:2). Elsewhere, Moses continues to emphasize the importance of what he is saying and its relevance for the future: 'Impress them on your children' (Deut. 6:7);

'Teach them to your children, talking about them when you sit at home and when you walk along the road, when you lie down and when you get up' (Deut. 11:19). Three times Moses stresses the importance of passing on the Word of God to future generations. Grasp the message. Earlier, when the people were being prepared for the exodus and were making ready the Passover meal, which was to be celebrated in perpetuity, Moses delivered a similar exhortation: 'And when your children ask you, "What does this ceremony mean to you?" then tell them ...' (Exod. 12:26–27). There seems to be an expectation, not only that the next generation must be told of God's actions on behalf of His people, but also that they will ask for an explanation (Deut. 32:7; Josh. 4:6).

SALVATION

Back to Paul's second letter to Timothy, and the first benefit of Scripture to which Paul draws our attention is that it opens the door to salvation through faith in Jesus Christ. Yes, it is the Holy Scriptures that make us wise to salvation (2 Tim. 3:15). It is in them that we learn of the intention of God: that forgiveness and mercy are offered to the world through the sacrifice of the Lamb, Jesus. The Word of God is the 'sword of the Spirit' (Eph. 6:17), which the Spirit uses to penetrate our minds and wills, 'soul and spirit, joints and marrow; it judges the thoughts and attitudes of the heart' (Heb. 4:12). It is by the living and active Word of God that the Spirit convicts 'the world of guilt in regard to sin and righteousness and judgment' (John 16:8–11). We may read helpful books or hear eloquent, enlightening sermons on the subject of salvation, but it is the 'God breathed' Word of God (2 Tim. 3:16), the Bible, which contains the good news of redemption in Jesus (2 Tim. 3:15).

CHRISTIAN LIVING AND MATURITY

But, having been brought into the knowledge of the saving grace of God in Jesus, there is then the necessity of learning how it ought to affect our lives. Finding Jesus, or, more correctly, being found by Him, is a beginning, not an end.

This is an important aspect in the whole picture of Christian maturity and living. One often gets the impression, perhaps wrongly, that some people, if they have been willing to give some consideration to Christian belief, are content with the saving work of God in Jesus. They are willing to say that they have become Christians, but it is often the 'hope of heaven', the wrongly perceived 'good life' or the protection and care that Jesus can bring that are the main attractions of faith. And there are plenty of preachers who are willing to proclaim that coming to Jesus will make everything OK. The necessity to change the direction of one's life, to amend one's lifestyle, is not portrayed as pleasing to God or enticing. We have to acknowledge that to follow Christ can at times be uncomfortable, and that is not a popular or easily acceptable notion. It is not all a bed of roses, and Jesus never promised that it would be. Indeed, He promised the opposite (John 15:20), but prayed for those exposed to the antagonism of the world (17:14–15). There are some thorns, and a study of the plight of some of our brethren living under hostile regimes today will very clearly bring this home to us. But to become a true disciple (Matt. 28:19), one's whole philosophy of life and living will need to change. To quote the apostle Paul in his second letter to the church in Corinth: 'if anyone is in Christ, he is a new creation' (2 Cor. 5:17). King David, in one of his psalms, pleaded with God to change him, to wash him, to cleanse him, to create in him a new heart (Ps. 51:7, 10). We cannot ignore the implications of Jesus' first miracle, when, at Cana in Galilee, He changed the water into wine (John 2:9). Change is obligatory if one is serious in one's Christian commitment—that is, if one is to adhere to Christ's command, 'Follow me', and love as He loved. Surely change is concomitant with repentance, the basis of our renewed relationship with God.

For guidance and instruction on this change within our lives, where do we turn? On the advice of the apostle Paul, we turn to the Scriptures. It is these which will train us in the way of righteousness (2 Tim. 3:16). They are able not only to teach us, but also to check our error and direct us along the right path, and to reveal the way of holiness. We must remember that God requires holiness of those who are His followers: 'Be holy, because I am holy' (1 Peter 1:16; Lev. 19:2). Holiness is God's will for us—that is, that we should be sanctified (1 Thes. 4:3).

The Christian faith is not a passive belief; it is not just believing dogma, but is an active faith. But neither is it just a system of behaviour—of being good! Embodied within our faith is a call not just to be good, but to do good. Discipleship should have a purpose, and that purpose, we read in 2 Timothy 3:17, is service! The Scriptures are not only to lead us into righteousness and a clearer understanding of our faith, but also to equip us to be active, profitable servants of Jesus, faithful witnesses (Acts 1:8) by word and work. God's people are to be prepared 'for works of service, so that the body of Christ may be built up' (Eph. 4:12). In Jesus' parable of the sheep and the goats, the commendation that included the offer 'Come ... take your inheritance' was extended to those who had 'done good' when seeing those in need: feeding the hungry, giving a drink to the thirsty, welcoming strangers, clothing the naked, caring for the sick and visiting prisoners (Matt. 25:34–36). Christianity is being and doing—not doing *in order* that we may be saved, but doing *because* we are saved.

If the church at Antioch was being well taught from the Scriptures (as we believe it was), and if the congregation was eager to learn from those Scriptures (as we believe they were), this short summary of Scripture's benefits explains why the church had an effective influence on the city. Why was it a growing church? In subsequent chapters we will see evidence that it was a well-taught fellowship which had responded positively to teaching. However, for ourselves, we should have grasped the importance of worshipping in a well-led church which should therefore be a well-fed church. The Bible is central for Christian well-being and growth: 'crave pure spiritual milk, so that by it you may grow up in your salvation' (1 Peter 2:2). There is much biblical ignorance abroad today; let us determine not to be part of it. The Lord warns that if we disregard the Word of God, He will create 'a famine of hearing the words of the LORD' (Amos 8:11).

TO THINK ABOUT

» How would you counsel someone who came for instruction on church membership, then afterwards attended church only occasionally?

» In some churches the sermon seems to be simplified to accommodate newcomers with little or no Bible understanding. How should mature Christians be fed in such a situation?

» How great a part should personal Bible reading and study play in deepening our own understanding of our faith and its outworking?

A worshipping church

While they were worshipping the Lord and fasting, the Holy Spirit said ... (Acts 13:2)

What is the most popular religious programme on television? There are not that many to choose from these days. It seems as if the programme planners have decided to sideline religion and exclude it from their schedules. Sunday worship services are not broadcast as regularly as they once were, and even at the major festivals of Christmas and Easter, not much prominence is given to their significance. This situation is in sharp contrast to the high profile that was given to Christian church worship on holy days in the past.

However, of the few television programmes of a Christian nature in the UK, I am sure you will have guessed that the most popular is *Songs of Praise*. Why should this be? After all, apart from the occasional interview or testimony, the programme consists of hymn-singing in various forms and in settings which vary from congregations gathered in traditional churches or cathedrals to more modern settings. Sometimes there is a soloist, at other times a duet, small group or choir. Whatever the setting or the format, the programmes are about hymn-singing, in which viewers are encouraged to participate by using the words shown on the screen. Indeed, some folk may judge the programme according to how many of the hymns they have known and been able to join in with. I would think that most viewers have had some connection with church, however tenuous or distant. I also have a suspicion that the average age of those who tune in each Sunday is well over fifty years, maybe over sixty. Of course, some viewers are unable to attend any service of worship and so, for them, the programme is a means of keeping in touch with their faith.

From this, we must not get the impression that it is only the older generations who appreciate hymnody. The proliferation of modern worship songs gives the lie to that assumption, as does the preponderance of CDs, DVDs and downloads featuring spiritual songs aimed at those from their teens to their twenties and upwards. We must conclude, then, that those with godly connections take pleasure in singing and listening to hymns and spiritual songs. There may be a cultural difference in preference which distinguishes between traditional hymns of a set metre and modern spiritual songs, but the basic fact remains: singing and music are an integral part of church life and Christian involvement. Indeed, singing Christian songs and hymns is generally referred to as 'worship'.

That last comment will offer a clue as to the third characteristic of the church at Antioch, which we are now about to consider. As well as being a well-led church and a well-fed church, we note that we are visiting a worshipping church (Acts 13:2). Therefore, in this chapter we will consider the relationship between hymn-singing and worship, as well as the attitude we must adopt if we are to be truly worshipping.

Music and worship

Although worship and praising God should be free of any contention, sadly it is often marred by, and can become a source of, strife. Churches that have a liturgical tradition seem to be particularly prone to discord on this subject. Occasionally the media will report that a clergyman is in dispute with the church organist, often supported by the choir, over the matter of church music. The congregation may take sides, and the issue is often about the introduction of modern hymnody and the use of different instruments. It is the ancient-versus-modern disagreement. This should not be so. Indeed, it seems to me that the newer non-denominational churches seem, for now, to be free of such controversy. However, there is no guarantee that they will not find themselves enmeshed in such arguments in the future. The crunch time seems to be a change of culture that involves music—a phenomenon that confirms the importance of hymns, and, in particular, the choice of hymns for worship. It reveals itself in those churches which as yet have not been able to succumb—or have no desire to yield—to PowerPoint. In these congregations, the hymn numbers are shown on the board at the front of church. Before the service starts, members of the congregation leaf through their hymn books to check the hymns that have been chosen—and, no doubt, mentally note their approval or otherwise of the musical selection. In more modern assemblies, the music seems to be played, and the congregation join in, with enthusiasm, in voice and physical movement.

So church people enjoy singing hymns and worship songs, and, regardless of tradition, singing as part of a large gathering can be moving and inspirational. But is it worship?

First, we have to concede that singing is an integral part of worship and praise. This is evident when we read the Old Testament Psalms, where we discover that praise and song are synonymous; for example: 'Sing to the LORD, praise his name' (Ps. 96:2); 'they believed his promises and sang his praise' (Ps. 106:12). True hymnody should enable us to praise God by singing. Generally, in order to praise, we have to sing. 'O Lord, open my lips, and my mouth will declare your praise' (Ps. 51:15).

However, it is possible to sing hymns and not be worshipping. This is evident in many ways. I recall an illustration from a sermon on Psalm 23 which I heard when I was young—you may have heard it too. An outstanding actor had recited this psalm in his usual excellent eloquence and on completion had been greeted by a grand ovation. Subsequently, he invited anyone from the audience who was familiar with the psalm to come onto the stage and do the recitation. An older man ascended onto the platform and began to read the familiar words: 'The LORD is my shepherd; I shall not want …' (KJV). At the end of the reading there was no applause—just complete silence, and also many eyes that dripped a tear. The old man, a little perplexed by the silent reception in contrast to that received by the elocutionist—not even a sympathetic clap—was reassured by the actor: 'The difference is,' he said, 'I know the psalm, but you know the Shepherd.' This is a reminder to us that worship is not just about knowing the songs, or even singing the songs, but about knowing the God to whom they are to be addressed. This is surely the essential point of worship: to know who we are worshipping, as well as why we are worshipping.

The who and why of worship

First, who we are worshipping? The simple, unadulterated answer—the correct answer—is God; to be a little more specific: the God of Abraham, Isaac and Jacob (Israel), the God and Father of our Lord Jesus Christ. He is not some distant mysterious, unfamiliar figure, or an idol, but a God who can be known (Gal. 4:9). When at the well outside Sychar Jesus spoke to the Samaritan woman about her spiritual need (John 4:5, 7), he informed her that the Samaritans worshipped what they did not know, in contrast to the Jews, who worshipped what they knew (4:22).

Therefore, as we come to worship, we need to be assured who it is we know and why He is deserving of our praise. For help we turn to the words of the apostle Paul at the start of his letter to the church at Ephesus: 'Praise be to the God and Father of our Lord Jesus Christ' (Eph. 1:3). This is very particular. And why? 'In him [Jesus Christ] we have redemption through his blood, the forgiveness of sins, in accordance with the riches of God's grace' (1:7).

The apostle Peter, in his first letter, begins in a similar vein. He too, like Paul, is in an attitude of worship as he writes and reveals to us quite clearly the who and the why of adoration: 'Praise be to the God and Father of our Lord Jesus Christ' (1 Peter 1:3). And why? Because 'In his great mercy he has given us new birth into a living hope through the resurrection of Jesus Christ from the dead' (1:4). These two great apostles are sure of the God whom they praise and worship, and if our adoration is to be genuine, we too must be assured as to the identity of the one to whom we offer praise, and why we do so. We worship the God and Father of Jesus Christ, whom He offered as the perfect sacrificial lamb for our salvation and forgiveness; so from thankful hearts we offer our sincere praise. If the church at Antioch can be described as being at worship, we can know assuredly that this was the direction and ground of their praise.

How should we worship?

If our hymn-singing is to be worship rather than the mere vocalization and chanting of words, if it is to be more than a pleasant musical exercise, we must not only be sure of who we addressing those words to and for what reason, but there must also be certain attitudes occupying our hearts and minds. In what manner should we come to worship?

To answer this question we go to that great worshipping example of the Old Testament, David, and turn to the Jews' hymn book, the Psalms. The Psalms of David have been used by God's people down through the centuries, and most of them are full of expressions of praise, which, of course, is why they are so relevant and helpful in allowing people to worship God in a genuine way. Words from this, the Old Testament hymn book, are the source of many of the hymns and worship songs we sing today.

JOY

Many examples could be chosen for our study, but we turn to the words of Psalm 122. From the opening verse we see that David has been invited to go to the temple and we read his response: 'I rejoiced with those who said to me, "Let us go to the house of the LORD"' (Ps. 122:1). David was glad, joyful, that he had the opportunity to go and worship God. One can almost picture David as he ascended the temple mount, going to share in the praise of God with his people, and going lightly, quickly, and in eager anticipation. David's eagerness was because he was going to worship God, not because he was going to the temple. There is a subtle difference.

While we must resist the temptation to belittle the benefit of a regular habit of going to church, we also need to remind ourselves that there is within us a temptation to descend into a rut with regard to church-going. It is Sunday, the day we go to church—so off we plod! We can all become susceptible to the danger of church attendance becoming a duty, a chore, a habit, not something we look forward to with anticipation. We need often to take time to reassess our approach to worship. For those in the more traditional churches, an opportunity for such an exercise is given during periods like Lent and Advent, but this need not be the only time we give the matter consideration. The result of so pondering should enable us to be like David and approach worship joyfully. Hopefully, as we come near to the church in Antioch and join the company of others who worship there, we will find ourselves drawn into a joyful anticipation of worship. And here is a final word from David: 'I love the house where you live, O LORD, the place where your glory dwells' (Ps. 26:8). What a heart for God, and for worship of Him!

GRATITUDE

As we further consider the matter of worship, we ask next: What should be our attitude as we come to worship God? For guidance on this we turn to words written by the apostle Paul to the church at Colossae. What should be the attitude of heart for these Christians as they worship, or, more particularly, as they 'sing psalms, hymns and spiritual songs' (Col. 3:16)? They, says Paul, should have 'gratitude in [their] hearts to God'. Paul is repeating himself here, because in the previous verse he has called the church to thankfulness in the context of their unity and peace (3:15). A grateful, thankful heart should be a natural characteristic if we take our minds back to what we briefly noted earlier in this chapter: that the reason for our worship includes the fact that, through the resurrection of Jesus, we have a great hope of eternity. We have been delivered from death through the cross. We have been saved (1 Peter 1:3). We have been forgiven (Eph. 1:7). And if through faith in Jesus we have realized the extent of our need, the depth of the love and sacrifice of Jesus, and our ultimate fate without Him—hell—we should be eternally grateful. Surely the import of our worship is to express our thanks to God for 'such a great salvation' (Heb. 2:3). As we are worshipping, then, we should adopt the manner and attitude of the psalmist, who proclaims, 'Worship the LORD with gladness; come before him with joyful songs ... Enter his gates with thanksgiving and his courts with praise; give thanks to him and praise his name' (Ps. 100:2, 4).

Some will wish to add that our gratitude should include thankfulness for God's daily provision. This is, of course, correct. We ought always to be grateful for the provision God gives for our daily sustenance: our food, our clothes, our homes, and all the other blessings of life. But we may be speaking from a comfortable Western environment, and may have to remind ourselves of the conditions which some of our less fortunate brothers and sisters in Christ have to endure. Many have meagre possessions and little food, and, thinly clothed, they live in squalid accommodation. This does not mean they are not thankful for what they have—indeed, when they have so little to begin with, they express deep thankfulness for what they do receive, however small. Their gratitude may even exceed and be more heartfelt than Western affluent Christianity can conceive. Comfortable Christians may consider that, materially, the Christians living in conditions of poverty have very little to be thankful for; but the evidence is that these brothers and sisters are still able to praise and worship God for their forgiveness and salvation through Jesus—by their zeal, putting comfortable Western Christianity to shame. Our brothers and sisters living in poverty and persecution reproach and rebuke us by their enthusiastic worship and the gratitude in their hearts.

HUMILITY

One of the central themes of the letter to the Hebrews is that Jesus is a High Priest after the order of Melchizedek. As High Priest He is now seated in heaven, interceding on our behalf (Heb. 7:25); and because of where He is, and because of His completed work, we can approach the throne of grace 'with confidence' (4:16). However, this does not mean that we can approach God—even come to worship Him—in self-confidence or arrogance. No; as we come to praise God it must be with humility.

You will recall the words spoken by God to Moses from the burning bush: 'Do not come any closer ... Take off your sandals, for the place where you are standing is holy ground' (Exod. 3:5). Throughout the Old Testament, and in the prophecy of Isaiah in particular, God is referred to as the Holy One of Israel (e.g. Isa. 5:19). This stress on God's holiness ought to be enough to reveal to us that our approach to God should be tempered with reverence and humility. Again, we turn to the Psalms for an example. In a psalm where the psalmist is encouraging the people to worship with joy and thanksgiving, he adds, 'Come, let us bow down in worship, let us kneel before the LORD our Maker' (Ps. 95:6). An attitude of submission and meekness is required before a holy, awesome God.

We observe a similar response from Isaiah when he realized he was in the presence of a holy God: 'Woe to me!' he cried; 'I am ruined! For I am a man of unclean lips, and I live among a people of unclean lips, and my eyes have seen the King, the LORD Almighty' (Isa. 6:5). He was completely humbled in the presence of the holy God.

The emphasis on humility before God is not confined to the Old Testament; in the New Testament too we discover a stress on reverence. The letter to the Hebrews exhorts us to 'worship God acceptably with reverence and awe' (Heb. 12:28). Three of the New Testament epistles exhort their readers to be humble. 'Humble yourselves before the Lord,' writes James (James 4:10). Peter, more succinctly, writes, 'Humble yourselves' (1 Peter 5:6). Whereas in these two instances the significance of the appeal may be our position before God, Paul's emphasis includes a humble attitude towards each other: 'Be completely humble and gentle;

be patient, bearing with one another in love' (Eph. 4:2). Both James and Peter stress that, as a response to our humility before Him, God will lift us up, exalt us (James 4:10; 1 Peter 5:6).

An attitude of humility before God is epitomized in the response of the Virgin Mary to His call to become the mother of His Son. Her response is, 'I am the Lord's servant ... May it be to me as you have said' (Luke 1:38). Subsequently in her psalm of praise, Mary reminds us that God has 'lifted up the humble', a thought reminiscent not only of James and Peter (see above), but also of the psalmist, who declares, 'He [God] crowns the humble with salvation' (Ps. 149:4).

The clearest example of humility before God is, of course, to be found in the life of Jesus. Paul, writing to the Philippians in that well-known passage (which is possibly a quote from an early hymn), reminds us that in descending from heaven to earth Jesus 'humbled himself' and became 'obedient to death' (Phil. 2:8). Furthermore, Jesus entreats those who are weary and burdened to find rest in Him, saying that He is 'gentle and humble in heart' (Matt. 11:29).

Genuine heart worship

So we have seen that as we approach God to worship Him it should be with an attitude of joyful praise, thanksgiving and humility. It may be true that we can consciously ponder such matters, exercising the mind, as part of a mental process of coming to worship. But, as noted earlier, worship which is purely cerebral may be nothing more than singing hymns and saying prayers, rather than actually worshipping and praying. I am reminded here of the old hymn, 'I often say my prayers, but do I ever pray?' (John Burton). Worship that is genuine worship comes not only from the mind and the mouth, but also from the heart. The prophet Isaiah puts this thought into words which express God's disappointment and sorrow at the worship of His people who imagine that they are worshipping, but who, says God, are uttering only empty words: 'These people come near to me with their mouth and honour me with their lips, but their hearts are far from me' (Isa. 29:13). In the New Testament, when Jesus is confronted by the Pharisees, who are fastidious and complain about the disciples dining without washing their hands, He accuses them of hypocrisy and quotes these verses to them (Matt. 15:8–9).

As we noted above, the Psalms are a great source of inspiration and guidance with regard to our approach to and the content of our worship. The matter of our heart, our soul, our spirit, being involved in our worship also emerges in this book of ancient hymns; for example: 'I will praise you, O LORD my God, with all my heart' (Ps. 86:12). In Psalm 103 the psalmist is effusive in his praise, and he knows whence this worship and adoration flow: from his soul, his innermost heart: 'Praise the LORD, O my soul,' he urges of himself not once, but three times (Ps. 103:1, 2, 22), at the beginning and the end of his hymn. The next psalm begins and ends in the same manner in a pleading for the soul to well up with worship: 'Praise the LORD, O my soul' (Ps. 104:1, 35). These few verses reveal to us that worship is not just a physical activity of the larynx and the lungs, but is of the heart too; it is something to do with our very being. Jesus confirmed this truth when speaking to the Samaritan woman. He told her that 'God is spirit, and his worshippers must worship in spirit and in truth' (John 4:24). Generally speaking, we do need words and music to facilitate our worship, but these are to enable us to express the feelings of the heart, not as an end in themselves. I am sure that this will be the form of the worship we will experience at the church in Antioch: earnest, heartfelt praise.

Worship like this flows naturally from hearts that are full of thanksgiving for what God has done for us through the sacrificial death of Jesus on the cross: our redemption by the grace of God, through the blood of Jesus. Earlier we reminded ourselves from 1 Peter 1:3 and Ephesians 1:7 that thanksgiving proceeds from a heart that knows such a salvation. The same verses are applicable to the issue of heartfelt praise too. You will recall that these two letters begin with praise, followed by clear details of the reason why: God has redeemed us!

Glorifying God

As well as offering praise to God, we worship in order to glorify Him. On occasions we ourselves will feel uplifted as we praise God, especially if we are gathered with a great crowd of fellow believers, but principally we do not gather to feel good ourselves, but to lift up the name of the Lord, to glorify God, to bring praise and honour to His name. We see this in two psalms attributed to David: 'Glorify the LORD with me: let us exalt his name together' (Ps. 34:3); 'I will glorify your name for ever' (Ps. 86:12b). To glorify God was also the desire of His Son, Jesus. As He was musing over His impending death, He uttered the phrase 'Father, glorify your name!' (John 12:28a). Miraculously, and unexpectedly, the voice of God responded from heaven: 'I have glorified it, and will glorify it again' (12:28b). This deep longing of Jesus for the glory of His Father is seen again in His pre-passion prayer, where He appeals for the Son to be glorified, that He 'may glorify you' (17:1). And even before His crucifixion and resurrection Jesus could claim to the Father, 'I have brought you glory on earth by completing the work you gave me to do' (17:4).

Worship and our daily lives

There is a dangerous trap into which it is easy to tumble with regard to worship. It is to develop the notion that worship is something we do when we meet together with other Christians on Sunday, or possibly when we gather in our home or cell groups. We may also consider that when we draw aside into our 'closet' for our personal time of meditation, prayer and adoration, we are worshipping then. This is, of course true, but these are all set, prepared times, whether corporate or personal, when we are particularly seeking to praise God. What of the rest of our lives? Is worship a switched-on time, and then, when it is over, we switch off? Not so!

Sometimes the implication is given that our whole lives should be an act of worship, a notion no doubt influenced by Paul's words to the church at Colossae, when he reminds them that the whole of life should be lived out in service of God: 'Whatever you do, work at it with all your heart, as working for the Lord, not for men' (Col. 3:23). So, indeed, our whole lives are to be an act of worship to God—obviously different from when we are singing hymns and worship songs, but still an act of worship. However, in order to come to a deeper understanding of what we are trying to grasp about this aspect of worship, let us consider two instances from the Old Testament. These two examples are negative in that they are occasions when God says the worship being offered is *not* acceptable, and the reason why is given.

UNACCEPTABLE WORSHIP

We turn first to some words uttered by the prophet Amos, where we find God most forceful in His words of rejection of the people's worship:

I hate, I despise your religious feasts;
  I cannot stand your assemblies.
Even though you bring me burnt offerings and grain offerings,
  I will not accept them ...
Away with the noise of your songs!
  I will not listen to the music of your harps.
(Amos 5:21–23)

One is left in no doubt as to God's dissatisfaction with the people's worship. What was wrong with it? The reason for God's condemnation is clearly evident from the subsequent appeal for justice (5:24). The worshippers' lives were marred by injustice. There was an inconsistency between their lives and their worship. Eventually the prophet details the particular problem. The people to whom these words were addressed were guilty of oppression, exploitation, corruption and abuse. They trampled the needy and the poor (8:4). But how? They said, 'When will the New Moon be over that we may sell grain, and the Sabbath be ended that we may market wheat?' (8:5a). And they were accused of

skimping the measure,
  boosting the price
  and cheating with dishonest scales,
buying the poor with silver
  and the needy for a pair of sandals,
selling even the sweepings with the wheat.
(8:5b–6)

These words confirm that any words spoken or attitudes adopted in worship are meaningless without a life governed by righteousness and justice.

It was not only the prophet Amos who was called to challenge the people's approach to worship. Isaiah was given the same responsibility, and from his utterances we see repeated the Lord's disapproval of insincere worship—that is, worship marred by an insensitive lifestyle. Isaiah's condemnation is perhaps even stronger than that of Amos. To start with, Isaiah equates his listeners with the inhabitants of the cities of Sodom and Gomorrah (Isa. 1:10) and then continues with stern criticism:

The multitude of your sacrifices—
  what are they to me? ...
I have no pleasure
  in the blood of bulls and lambs and goats ...
Stop bringing meaningless offerings!

Your incense is detestable to me ...
I cannot bear your evil assemblies.
Your New Moon festivals and your appointed feasts
my soul hates.
They have become a burden to me ...
When you spread out your hands in prayer,
I will hide my eyes from you;
even if you offer many prayers,
I will not listen.
(1:11–15)

These are strong words of disapproval and denunciation from God. I wonder if, when we are heartily singing our hymns and praying, perhaps with some ignored error in the background, we ever consider that our worship may not be acceptable to God; that our iniquities are separating us from Him, and our sins have hidden His face from us (Isa. 59:2). The reason for Isaiah's words of condemnation includes hands stained with blood; evil deeds; wrongs; injustice; oppression; and a reluctance to consider the needs of widows and orphans (1:15–17). This covers a wide range of godlessness, and is a further clear reminder that worship of God carries responsibilities. Adoration and praise are worthless unless they come from hearts that are seeking to live in accordance with His will. No doubt that is why the Reformers, drawing up their liturgies, ensured that they commenced with confession and penitence. In this way they sought to ensure that the heart was cleansed so that the ensuing worship was genuine.

Finally, we turn to the well-known words of Paul written to the church at Rome. He urges his readers to live out their lives as acts of worship: 'I urge you, brothers, in view of God's mercy, to offer your bodies as living sacrifices, holy and pleasing to God—this is your spiritual act of worship' (Rom. 12:1). Surely he is saying here that our lives are to be part of our act of worship. Our singing of praise to God has to find continuance in our daily living, in living acts of worship that are an acceptable sacrifice before God. Such acts of worship are, of course, not the same as our praising God in song and prayer; it means living lives in a worshipful, God-honouring way. The 'Prayer of General Thanksgiving' in the Anglican Prayer Book sets out quite clearly this link between our worship and our lives: 'that we shew forth thy praise, not only with our lips, but in our lives; by giving up ourselves to thy service, and by walking before thee in holiness and righteousness all our days.'[1]

Mutual encouragement

It should be obvious to us that genuine, heart-felt, thankful praise is no less than God deserves, but the apostle Paul reminds us that true worship can also have healthy consequences for others. To be gathered together with fellow believers and to be taken along in joyful praise to God can be an uplifting experience. Being assembled among a great crowd of voices praising God in vibrant singing is a great encouragement to all those gathered. The writer of the letter to the Hebrews confirms that this ought to be one of the benefits of our meeting together: 'Let us not give up meeting together, as some are in the habit of doing, but let us encourage one another' (Heb. 10:25). Christians will be greatly encouraged by each other's presence as they are united in worship.

But what about any effect such corporate praise of God might have on any unbelievers who are present? In his first letter to the Corinthians, where Paul is giving instruction with regard to the conduct of worship, he makes reference to this possibility. Principally he is delivering teaching with regard to prophecy and speaking in tongues, and the relevance or otherwise to believers and unbelievers (1 Cor. 14:22–25), but in the closing verse of this section he notes the effect of the worship of that fellowship on an unbeliever: 'and the secrets of his heart will be laid bare. So he will fall down and worship God, exclaiming, "God is really among you!"' (1 Cor. 14:25). I am sure that our sincere worship would have the same effect. As we have noted, members of the church at Antioch earned the sobriquet 'Christian'. Perhaps it was their worship and their consequent lifestyles that had some influence on this understanding!

Worship in heaven

As we approach the fellowship of believers at Antioch to share in their worship, and having pondered what true worship involves, there is one further matter of which we need to be aware. Think about this question: What do you consider is one of the main activities in heaven? Did you answer 'Worship'? That response would surely be correct, as John, in Revelation, opens a window into heaven for us to reveal this truth. In this glimpse into the Holy of Holies we see myriads of angels, the living creatures and the elders bowing down in worship before the throne of God and the Lamb. They are accompanied by a multitude that no one can number, who sing the songs of heaven (Rev. 4:9–10; 5:8, 11–12, 14; 7:9, 11).

They sing,

Holy, holy, holy
is the Lord God Almighty. (Rev. 4:8)

You are worthy, our Lord and God. (4:11)

You are worthy ...
because you were slain. (5:9)

Worthy is the Lamb. (5:12)

To him who sits on the throne and to the Lamb
be praise and honour and glory and power. (5:13)

Amen!
Praise and glory. (7:12)

From these few references we see that heaven is full of praise and worship to God and to the Lamb. Worship, then, is a principal activity in heaven, so when we are sharing in praise here on earth we are simultaneously uniting with the great choirs in heaven. There are some who would say that praising God and Jesus in our church worship is but practice for the real thing, the time when we will be in the presence, and accepted into membership, of the heavenly chorus, sharing in worship with the angels, the elders and the living creatures assembled around the throne.

As a final reminder of the importance of worship of God we need to recall some words Jesus spoke to the Pharisees. On the occasion of His triumphal entry into Jerusalem, when He rode on an ass, the Pharisees implored Him to bid His disciples to desist in praise. His reply was significant: 'I tell you ... if they keep quiet, the stones will cry out' (Luke 19:40). If no one else had praised Jesus, or understood that the occasion warranted great rejoicing, the very stones on the ground would have burst forth in adoration.

As we share in the worship of the church at Antioch, immersed in and transported by the praise of the congregation, we may not be conscious of the various elements of a genuine worshipping heart, but I am sure that deep within each of their hearts there will be an inner awareness of all that God means to them, which reveals itself in their earnest, exuberant voices.

Enter his gates with thanksgiving
    and his courts with praise;
give thanks to him and praise his name.

For the LORD is good and his love endures for ever;
his faithfulness continues through all generations.
(Ps. 100:4–5)

To think about

- Do you think some folk turn up at church to worship, without any consideration why? How can we ensure we come to worship reverently?
- What might be hindrances to our worship?
- Is it necessary to be conscious, every time we worship, of the elements of worship we have considered?
- Are there things we can do to aid the worship of our own fellowship?

NOTE

1 Church of England, *Book of Common Prayer,* 'Prayers and Thanksgivings', https://www.churchofengland.org/prayer-worship/worship/book-of-common-prayer/prayers-and-thanksgivings.aspx.

A praying church

While they were worshipping the Lord and fasting, the Holy Spirit said, 'Set apart for me Barnabas and Saul for the work to which I have called them.' So after they had fasted and prayed, they placed their hands on them and sent them off. (Acts 13:2–3)

As well as being a well-led, well-taught, worshipping church, we also see that the church at Antioch was a praying church. It was a church that took praying seriously enough that they accompanied prayer and worship with fasting. Not only do we discover that the Holy Spirit spoke clearly to them during prayer, indicating that they should commission Barnabas and Paul for missionary endeavour, but we see also that before sending them out on their travels there was a time of valedictory prayer.

Perhaps we take it for granted that prayer is an important and concomitant part of Christian experience and life. However, prayer in public, like private prayer, is not without its difficulties. If there were any such tensions at Antioch they are not recorded. We read only that, when they were together, they prayed, and they were evidently a praying, prayerful church.

Imagine that you were gathered with a company of others listening to teaching on the subject of prayer. If, before the instruction began, you were asked without warning to lead the assembly in prayer, how would you respond? Now there will be some who are experienced enough to react to the request carefully, confidently and sensitively, but I imagine that for others, such a request would cause some consternation and trepidation. Is that you? I know that the first time I was asked to open in prayer, without prior warning, it was the cause of some perturbation—gulp! I was familiar with praying extemporarily, but that out-of-the-blue request took me off guard. I managed to blurt out some words, hopefully appropriately, and, having been called upon several times since, I hope that I can now respond to any such request calmly and prayerfully in the Spirit.

Now imagine that you were gathered with others and the request was made for you all to spend some time in extempore prayer in a group. Would silence reign? Here again there would be some who would be able to respond confidently, but there would also be many who would be overcome with self-consciousness and be 'tongue-tied'. This is not to be critical, but simply to highlight the fact that corporate prayer does not come easily.

I have a sneaking suspicion that, when the church at Antioch was said to be fasting and praying (Acts 13:2–3), it was the whole church and not just a few members—such as the prophets and teachers, or, in modern parlance, the so-called 'superspiritual'! Likewise, after Jesus' ascension into heaven, the disciples gathered in the Upper Room and we read that they all joined together constantly in prayer (Acts 1:14).

Antioch was thus a praying church, and we must consider that prayer ought to be an ordinary, normal, expected church occupation, the activity of assembled Christians.

Do we need to pray together?

I am aware that formal prayer is exercised in some church services and meetings, and it appears that Paul is giving some instruction in this area as he writes to Timothy (1 Tim. 2:1–2). Here Paul's request for prayer is very broad: "intercession … be made for everyone," highlighting the necessity of intercession for government and the peoples of the world. As we consider the urgent needs of our world today, we can appreciate how essential are such petitions. Such prayer during formal worship faithfully heeds Paul's exhortation.

Also, Jesus quite clearly teaches that we must spend time in prayer alone, and we get the impression that this ought to be a regular activity, a withdrawal from the world's distractions to a private place where we can speak with our Heavenly Father (Matt. 6:6). In no way is it right to undermine or disregard formal and personal private prayer, which are indeed important and part of the prayer life of a church. But isn't extempore prayer, made audibly in a formal church service, small group or prayer meeting, an area where some of us are reticent? It is in this area that disquiet and hesitation are often evidenced. So why should Christians pray aloud together?

THE EXAMPLE OF THE EARLY CHURCH

A simple, straightforward answer to this question is because the disciples and members of the early church community did so. We have already seen how, post-ascension, the disciples were all at prayer (Acts 1:14). We read that on the Day of Pentecost the disciples were again all together in one place, and because of the descent of the Holy Spirit on their gathering we can assume they were at prayer (2:1). Also, when Peter and John were released after their arrest by the Sanhedrin, they joined the others, where they all raised their voices in prayer (4:24). On this occasion too we read that the Holy Spirit descended among them and empowered them with great boldness (4:31). On a subsequent occasion, when Peter was led out miraculously from prison by an angel, he went to the house of Mary, mother of John Mark, where he found many people gathered together and praying (12:12). After the events of the Day of Pentecost, when three thousand people came to believe in Jesus (2:41), we are informed that one of the activities these new converts were devoted to was prayer (2:42), along with the apostles' teaching, the fellowship and the breaking of bread.

For one further example we go to the beach at the port of Miletus. Paul was heading for Jerusalem and an uncertain future. He called the elders of the church at Ephesus to assemble at Miletus and, after his farewell oration and exhortation, they knelt to pray—right there on the beach (Acts 20:36).

NEW TESTAMENT TEACHING ON PRAYER

Of course, examples carry much weight on any subject, but it is also helpful to hear of the teaching that authenticates the experience. The key reference in this respect must be the oft-quoted words of Jesus wherein He promises to be present when, at the minimum, two or three are gathered in His name and are in agreement with regard to the request (the prayer) that is being offered (Matt. 18:19–20). Although this is not a direct instruction, there is the implication, even the expectation, that His followers will together want to communicate with Him in prayer.

Further evidence of Jesus' expectation that the disciples would wish to continue making requests of Him is revealed among His last words to the disciples, as recorded by the apostle John: 'I will do whatever you ask in my name, so that the Son may bring glory to the Father. You may ask me for anything in my name, and I will do it' (John 14:13–14); 'my Father will give you whatever you ask in my name. Until now you have not asked for anything in my name. Ask and you will receive, and your joy will be complete' (John 16:23–24; see also Matt. 7:7). In a different way, in the Garden of Gethsemane Jesus urged the disciples to pray (Matt. 26:41; Mark 14:38; Luke 22:40). In all these instances we may assume that Jesus wished and expected them to be together, and united in prayer. Jesus was not so much teaching them to pray, but encouraging them to do so.

At the end of some of Paul's epistles we see that he includes a plea for the church to pray for him and his ministry. As his letters would have been read to the congregation, no doubt gathered together to hear what Paul had to say, we can again assume that his request was that, at times, they ought to pray together. He writes, for example, 'always keep on praying for all the saints. Pray also for me' (Eph. 6:18–19); 'by prayer and petition, with thanksgiving, present your requests to God' (Phil. 4:6); 'Devote yourselves to prayer' (Col. 4:2).

One day when Jesus was praying, one of His disciples approached Him and asked, 'Lord, teach us to pray' (Luke 11:1). I believe this reveals that the disciples of Jesus had a natural desire to pray. And not only was it a request for guidance on prayer, but it was also a plea to be guided on the content of prayer. We know this because by way of an answer Jesus gave the pattern for prayer which we incorporate into our liturgies as the Lord's Prayer (Luke 11:2–4).

The benefits of praying together

If our contact with the prayerful church at Antioch has helped us to consider the necessity of praying together, let this contact also help us to consider the benefits of corporate prayer (this is not, of course, to imply that there is no benefit and blessing from private and formal prayers).

We have already mentioned in passing Jesus' word regarding the benefit of at least two or three praying together: He promises to be present (Matt. 18:19–20). But as well as the promise of His presence, there is also the promise of a positive answer in response to a request. This is dependent on agreement on the matter being asked for: 'if two of you on earth agree about anything you ask for, it will be done for you by my Father in heaven.' Praying together in agreement carries the promise of answered prayer, and praying aloud in the presence of others gives them the opportunity to assert their unity with prayer requests. This is illustrated in the Old Testament when David, who had overseen the eventual return of the Ark of the Covenant to Jerusalem, burst forth into a psalm of praise, and committed it to Asaph and his associates (1 Chr. 16:7). When they came to the end of the psalm, all the people added their acclamation: 'Then all the people said, "Amen" and "Praise the LORD."' There was a close unity.

We have also already mentioned the prayer of the church at Jerusalem following the release of Peter and John from prison (Acts 4:23–31). Not only can we use this resultant prayer meeting as an example of praying together, but we also see that it contained the blessing of drawing the people close together: 'they raised their voices together in prayer' (4:24); and we discover that, as a result of their prayer and unity, the Lord responded in a miraculous way: 'After they prayed ... they were all filled with the Holy Spirit and spoke the word of God boldly' (4:31). One senses that there was at this point a deep sense of fellowship and unity among them.

As the apostle Paul approaches the end of his epistle to the Galatians he urges them to 'Carry each other's burdens' (Gal. 6:2). We can be assured that one way in which he would have us bear each other's burdens is through the medium of prayer. As we have noted, Paul ends some of his letters with a plea for his readers to be prayerful. Sometimes he is more specific and requests prayer for himself, for his ongoing ministry and the faithful proclamation of the gospel. To the Ephesians he declares, 'Pray ... for me, that whenever I open my mouth, words may be given me so that I will fearlessly make known the mystery of the gospel, for which I am an ambassador in chains. Pray that I may declare it fearlessly, as I should' (Eph. 6:19–20). He takes the same approach as he ends his epistle to the church at Colossae, soliciting their prayers for his preaching of the message of Christ: 'pray for us, too, that God may open a door for our message ... Pray that I may proclaim it clearly, as I should' (Col. 4:3–4). When writing to the church in Thessalonica the first time he simply pleads, 'pray for us' (1 Thes. 5:25), expanding this in his second letter: 'pray for us that the message of the Lord may spread rapidly, and be honoured, just as it was with you' (2 Thes. 3:1). Elsewhere Paul also asks for prayer that he 'may be rescued from the unbelievers in Judea' (Rom. 15:31) and that he may be 'delivered from wicked and evil men' (2 Thes. 3:2). Not that Paul's approach to prayer is one-sided: as he pens most of his letters he begins with the assurance that he prays for those to whom he is writing (Eph. 1:16; Phil. 1:4, 9; Col. 1:3; 2 Thes. 1:11–12, etc.).

Praying together is a way in which we can share one another's burdens: the burden of spreading the gospel, and the burden of combating the evil and wicked atmosphere that surrounds us. It is a means whereby we can 'rejoice with those who rejoice [and] mourn with those who mourn' (Rom. 12:15).

We are truly bidden to pray together for one another, for God's people and worldwide work, for those in need, for world leaders, and so on. Some may be shy, nervous and self-conscious, or feel that they are not very eloquent (you have Moses for company, Exod. 4:10); others may lack confidence, are fearful of saying the wrong thing or are discouraged because someone has interceded on the subject that they had in mind to pray for. These are all genuine concerns and hindrances, but we need to try to remember that we are speaking to God our Heavenly Father, who longs to hear and answer our requests, and that we are in the company of our brothers and sisters in Jesus. Our joint fellowship in Christ should be a place of trust and freedom for prayer, and judgemental attitudes should be non-existent.

We may have gained the impression that our prayers must be lengthy and involved, but this is not the case. Indeed, I am often amazed at the effectiveness of prayers in the Bible which are brief and to the point. The prayer of Elijah on Mount Carmel is one that stays in my mind (1 Kings 18:36–37). In the text, the prayer is two verses long, yet the immediate outcome was fire that consumed even a water-drenched sacrifice. Elijah was brief, praying for something that was a concern of his heart. Equally, it could not be said that the Lord's Prayer is very long and detailed. Hopefully, such examples can be an encouragement to us in our praying together.

The church at Antioch was a praying church, a prayerful church. They almost certainly were a people who were involved in private prayer, setting aside time to be alone with God—which may not have been easy for them, especially if some of them were slaves. However, I believe the words at the beginning of Acts 13 emphasize that they also prayed together. May we be involved in churches which offer the opportunity for the congregation to pray together and where all feel free to participate.

To think about

- » Do you find it difficult to pray aloud with others? If so, why? Has this chapter helped address any fears you might have?
- » How can your fellowship encourage the practice of praying together?

An evangelistic church

... a great number of people were brought to the Lord. Then Barnabas went to Tarsus to look for Saul ... So for a whole year Barnabas and Saul met with the church and taught great numbers of people. (Acts 11:24–26)

While they were worshipping the Lord and fasting, the Holy Spirit said, 'Set apart for me Barnabas and Saul for the work to which I have called them.' So after they had fasted and prayed, they placed their hands on them and sent them off. (13:2–3)

Statistics. Counting numbers. This is a common activity today. From large retail conglomerates comparing like-for-like sales so that any rise or decline can be monitored (because it will affect their share value), to small, struggling churches: statistics are important, or so it seems. Although church attendance figures may have no influence on the Stock Exchange, nor are they likely to have any effect on the economy, they are of enough importance in church life to justify the publication of detailed church surveys revealing current attendance trends. Number-watching is a regular church occupation. 'How many come?' is a question frequently posed by people inquiring about a particular church—although, more correctly, in many instances this should be phrased 'How few attend?' But whether it is struggling churches bemoaning their lack of numbers, or the new 'mega-congregations' confident in their abundance, it seems that everyone is into number-watching and, in some cases, number-manipulation. Nevertheless, although not everyone is convinced by the accuracy of some statistical observations, there can be no doubting the decline in overall church membership in the UK, and the consequent need for concern and to wrestle with this issue.

Declining church attendance

There are those who are seeking earnestly and prayerfully to rectify this downward spiral, and who are examining many courses that centre on the subject of church growth. There are also examples of thriving churches, with thousands on their rolls, who are open to sharing with others the underlying strategies of their 'success'. Many of these churches are in the USA, and attempts have been made to copy their so-called formulae for growth. Books and courses abound. Of course, some churches on this side of the Atlantic are also seeing signs of increase. Yet, although there are gleams of light in an otherwise gloomy situation, we need to accept and acknowledge that the general trend is diminishing attendance. Therefore these hated statistics ought to impel us to ask if there is anything that can be done to reverse this downward direction.

Much of the decline seems to be centred around the older, traditional denominations, whereas it is the newer, cross-denominational assemblies, sometimes termed 'non-denominational', which seem to be experiencing signs of increased membership. This must cause us not only to ask where the older denominations may be failing, but also to try to discern what God is doing. Have they perhaps fulfilled their usefulness? Is God is looking to a new way of proclaiming His word and truth? Or is it simply that age has brought complacency, and there is truly a need for a change of direction, or even a return to a vigorous and rigorous faith of former days?

There is no simple answer to this problem of declining church attendance, but as we look at the thriving church at Antioch, perhaps we ought to consider their approach. Not only are they a Scripture-fed, worshipping and praying church, but we also see that they are an evangelistic church. We see that, under the ministry and likely pastoral care and guidance of Barnabas and Paul, a great number of people were brought to the Lord (Acts 11:24–26). We also note that it was from this church that the Lord called out Barnabas and Paul to be sent on the first recorded missionary journey, which took the gospel to new lands and peoples—Cyprus, Pamphylia and Pisidia (Acts 13:2–4). So here at Antioch we should discover some help in tackling the issue of church decline/growth.

Reasons for church decline

First we need to consider whether we can discern any noticeable reason why church growth does not happen and why there is decline. There are at least two common reactions to decline.

SELF-PRESERVATION

First we start to look inwards, to a concern about our congregation, which naturally leads to a yearning for self-preservation. How will we survive? We do not wish to see our church close, so the temptation is to be inward-looking—which usually results in further decline, because we become unconcerned about anyone else.

A CLIQUE MENTALITY

Another problem, perhaps one which will exist before we become interested in self-preservation, is an unawareness of others for a different reason: the church has become a cosy clique. This can easily happen if people have been worshipping together for many years and have developed deep bonds of friendship and fellowship. Naturally, when they meet, they will greet each other warmly and engage in animated conversation. It is all very comforting and pleasant. But to a stranger, someone coming to worship, perhaps for the first time, it can project the notion of exclusivism, of a clique into which it is very difficult to break. In these two situations, maybe unintentionally, others are excluded, and the impression can be given that church is a closed shop unless you know someone, and that it is not interested in outreach.

LACK OF LOVE FOR THE LOST

But also, sadly, one of the reasons for falling membership could be that we have lost our concern for the lost. I must admit that more than ever I get the impression that the lost do not wish to be found, and constant rebuff and rejection can be both discouraging and off-putting. The natural reaction to such a response is to stop trying, but our commission from the Lord is to seek out the lost just as He did. Have we lost our evangelistic zeal? One of the inherent dangers of introversion and self-preservation is that our deepest concern, or principal source of disquiet, is getting people to come to church. It becomes our main aim. But this is purely a secondary aspect of the problem. Church attendance should be subsequent to conversion, not the other way round—although it does often work in that direction. For example, Paul did not seek out Christian fellowship until after he had been converted. Indeed, you may recall that the church was reluctant to admit him, and only did so thanks to the intervention of Barnabas (Acts 9:26–28). The approach today seems to be to bring people to church in order to introduce them to Christ. Perhaps this is a sign that we have lost the will for personal involvement in outreach.

It is possible that we have lost our concern for the lost in the two areas in which the church at Antioch was involved, namely locally and worldwide. Not just in individual churches, but, in the traditional churches at least, the church as a whole has lost its evangelistic fervour. Perhaps it can be argued that, generally speaking, the church has rarely had any evangelistic fervour. Encouraging people to become members of a church or the church, yes; but going forth in boldness to preach the Good News to the lost—well, that was probably the preserve of just one party of the church (or parachurch organizations and missionary societies). But they too have now lost their emphasis on this area of the church's ministry and mission. Once, those who were of an evangelical inclination were fervent with regard to evangelism. They would support evangelistic campaigns, organize parish missions and keenly support overseas missions. Many of the clergy were prepared for ordination at an evangelical missionary-society sponsored college—Bible Chuchmen's Missionary Society (BCMS; now part of TrinityCollege, Bristol). I sometimes wonder if such enthusiasm for evangelism still exists. There may be some question as to whether evangelistic crusades, of the type led by Billy Graham, are appropriate these days, but local and world mission is still necessary. It has to be said, though, that mission is now two-way, and Christians from abroad are coming to share the gospel in the UK, and no doubt to other countries that once sent out missionaries.

Let us then, at this point, consider the background to evangelism and its necessity, up to and including the church at Antioch.

The background to evangelism

First we remind ourselves of the mission aspect of Jesus' incarnation. When the Canaanite woman came to Jesus and pleaded with Him to have mercy on her daughter, who was possessed by a demon, He was specific in His reply, saying He had come to bring the Good News to the lost sheep of Israel (Matt. 15:24). In his letter to the church in Rome, Paul added more detail to the purpose of Christ's coming and mission: 'Christ has become a servant of the Jews on behalf of God's truth, to confirm the promises made to the patriarchs', with a spin-off for the rest of the world: 'so that the Gentiles may glorify God for his mercy' (Rom. 15:8–9; see also 1:16; 2:9–10). We read also that when Jesus sent out on mission His twelve disciples, it was with the instruction that they go 'to the lost sheep of Israel' (Matt. 10:6).

Jesus' mission was to bring the gospel of salvation primarily to His own people, the Jews, and then to the Gentiles (see also Luke 2:32, in the song of Simeon). However, before His life and mission were fulfilled on the cross, we see that His message of salvation was not exclusively for the Jews. During His sermon on the good shepherd, the sheep and the gate, he adds, 'I have other sheep that are not of this sheep pen. I must bring them also' (John 10:16). In the Great Commission, after His resurrection and prior to His ascension, Jesus' command to his followers is to 'go': 'Go and make disciples of all nations' (Matt. 28:20). When Luke records this exhortation in the Acts of the Apostles he is very specific with regard to the places where the gospel is to be proclaimed: 'Jerusalem ... Judea and Samaria, and to the ends of the earth' (Acts 1:8). In other words, the command was to share the gospel of salvation in Jesus at home and abroad.

Jesus' ministry was a teaching, preaching ministry. On one occasion when He returned to Nazareth and taught in the synagogue there He used words from the prophecy of Isaiah (Isa. 61:1–2) as the text for His sermon. The words from these verses reveal quite clearly the purpose of Jesus' incarnation: 'The Spirit of the Lord is on me, because he has anointed me to preach good news to the poor' (Luke 4:18). The subsequent verses reveal other aspects of the ministry of the Messiah, but the first aspect was to preach the Good News: 'The kingdom of God is near. Repent and believe the good news!' (Mark 1:15). Jesus incarnate was the Good News, and He preached the Good News.

Jesus came 'preaching the good news of the kingdom' (Matt. 4:23) and commanded His disciples to do the same: 'Go ... and preach the good news' (Mark 16:15); soon after His departure we see them going out in obedience to this injunction. We find the disciples, immediately upon receiving the Holy Spirit on the Day of Pentecost, preaching boldly in Jerusalem (Acts 2:5–6). They were preaching Jesus Christ and Him crucified (1 Cor. 1:23). Christ was the message. Their preaching had astounding results: three thousand people responded in faith and baptism (Acts 2:41). This was not an isolated case, of course, and the Acts of the Apostles is the ongoing story of the proclamation of the gospel. The promulgation of the gospel began in Jerusalem with the Jews, but before long the gospel was being announced in Judea, Samaria and to the ends of the world. The word was carried to the Gentiles—though not without some persuasion from the Holy Spirit, who used the martyrdom of Stephen to move the church out of Jerusalem (Acts 8:1) and a dream to stir up Peter (10:9–23). But to the Gentiles the apostles went: Peter to Cornelius at Caesarea and others to Phoenicia, Cyprus and Antioch (Acts 11). These evangelistic endeavours were granted success. For Peter, at the home of Cornelius, the household was touched by God (10:44–48), whilst at Antioch we see that the preaching had a far wider effect: 'a great member of people believed and turned to the Lord' (11:21). So we observe that, as well as Peter fulfilling the Great Commission, the church at Antioch started to be obedient to this directive too.

It is an interesting fact that, although the church at Antioch was formed out of evangelistic mission, evangelistic activity did not cease at this point. After the arrival of Barnabas from Jerusalem, outreach into the town must have continued as we read of a further great number of people being brought to the Lord (Acts 11:24). This example of local evangelism was eventually complemented by a more widespread outreach. Eventually this church became the precursor of overseas mission for the Christian church. It was from here that Paul and Barnabas were called out by the Holy Spirit and sent out on the first missionary journey (Acts 13:2–3). We can conjecture that evangelistic concern had been the core of their prayer (Acts 13:2), and it was in answer to that prayer that the Holy Spirit called out two of their leaders for such a ministry.

Evangelism and church services: the early church model

As mentioned above, because of the evidence that church attendance is in decline, there is a danger that we concentrate our efforts on trying to persuade people to come to church. There is a temptation to present church, even the songs sung in worship, as 'entertaining', in this respect. However, this is not really the aim of evangelism. In the early church, outreach to unbelievers would not necessarily take place as part of worship, or in the context of worship. Worship was when and where the believers met together to praise God and be encouraged in faith (Acts 20:7). It was an exclusively Christian activity. The only indication that any unbelievers might be present is found in Paul's first letter to the Corinthians: 'But if an unbeliever or someone who does not understand comes in ...' (1 Cor. 14:24). Note that this is only a possibility—'if'—and perhaps a remote one at that.

We do not evangelize to bring people to church, but to reveal Jesus to them, to seek to lead them to faith. I am sure that the church in Antioch had a prayerful desire to lead people to Jesus, and as a result their church was well attended. Also I believe that as long as a church maintains a concern for the lost and is involved in prayerful outreach, locally and abroad, God will continue to use it to the glory of His name and the extension of His kingdom.

The how and why of evangelism

As we move to consider the how and why of evangelism, let us first remind ourselves of why any of us needs to hear the gospel message. This, of course, includes ourselves.

WHY EVANGELIZE?

Why did Jesus have to come and eventually die on a cross? This surely is a major question as we seek to explain the purpose of evangelism. Both Peter and Paul tell us quite clearly the answer to this question. Although the two apostles use different words, they offer the same reason. Peter, in his first epistle, says quite simply it was 'to bring [us] to God' (1 Peter 3:18). These words are written in the context of discussing Christ's atoning sacrifice for sin. The sacrificial death of Christ is also the context of Paul's words to the church at Corinth: 'God was reconciling the world to himself in Christ' (2 Cor. 5:19). The implication behind these words, especially 'reconciling', is that the relationship between God and His creation, mankind, has been torn asunder. Paul describes this situation as he writes to the Ephesian church: 'separate from Christ ... without hope and without God in the world' (Eph. 2:12); 'separated from the life of God because of the ignorance that is in them due to the hardening of their hearts' (4:18). We seek to be involved in evangelism because mankind is separated from its Creator, God, because of sin, but Jesus has dealt with this severance through His sacrificial death. This is stated quite clearly by Paul in his first letter to Timothy: 'Christ Jesus came into the world to save sinners' (1 Tim. 1:15).

In our unregenerate state we are like sheep without a shepherd (Matt. 9:36), like sheep whom the Good Shepherd (John 10:11) wants to seek out (Luke 15:4). Whether or not we are able to admit to our separation, our lostness, that is the reality according to the Word of God. It is the reality of being lost that drives one to seek salvation. So why do we evangelize? It is to bring the lost to the Good Shepherd.

We need to be sure that we fully appreciate the condition of the lost—what it means to be 'without hope and without God in the world' (Eph. 2:12). Paul emphasizes this condition clearly at the beginning of that chapter: 'dead in your transgressions and sins' (Eph. 2:1). The apostle John, in both his Gospel and his first epistle, says quite clearly that life is a gift from God through His Son, Jesus, and that faith in Him gives life; but those who reject Him 'will not see life, for God's wrath remains on him' (John 3:36); such a person 'does not have life' (1 John 5:12). In his vision of the end times John paints a graphic, fearsome picture of the fate of those whose names are not written in the Book of Life: they are 'thrown into the lake of fire' (Rev. 20:15).

The outlook is dire and should be sufficient stimulation for our proclamation of the Good News. Sadly, however, complacency and apathy overtake us, so we need some further stimuli for evangelism.

First, as we have already noted, we are commanded to go—and by none other than Jesus Himself in His last words to His disciples: 'go and make disciples of all nations' (Matt. 28:19); 'you will be my witnesses' (Acts 1:8). We must evangelize—share with others the good news of the saving grace of God in Jesus Christ—because Jesus commands us to do so.

Secondly, we see that God has deputed to us the responsibility to proclaim His reconciliatory act in Jesus. He has made us His representatives, His ambassadors, to spread the Good News. The apostle Paul classifies himself as an ambassador (in chains; Eph. 6:20), but in his second letter to the Corinthians he uses the plural: 'gave us the ministry of reconciliation ... We are therefore Christ's ambassadors' (2 Cor. 5:18, 20).

Thirdly, we share the Good News because we have experienced its blessing for ourselves. This takes us back to what we looked at above concerning our state as lost, separated from God, dead in trespasses and sins, without God and without hope. If we have come to realize our lostness outside of God, have responded to the invitation to repent and believe the gospel (Mark 1:15) and thus know the peace and grace of forgiveness, we should want to share this Good News. We see a clear example of this in the encounter between Peter and his brother Andrew. Andrew and another, unnamed, disciple had been introduced to Jesus through their association with John the Baptist (John 1:35–39). We then read that the first thing Andrew did was to search out Peter and speak those well-known words, 'We have found the Messiah' (1:41); he then brought his brother to Jesus (1:42). We see that Andrew's stimulation for evangelism was that he had found and met the Christ. The next incident that John records in his Gospel is similar. This time it is Philip who announces to his sceptical friend Nathaniel, 'We have found the one Moses wrote about in the Law' (1:45).

So, although our knowledge that those who are without Christ, whose names are not written in the Book of Life, are in danger of being cast into the lake of fire (Rev. 20:15) should be sufficient incentive for us to evangelize, we find that the Scriptures offer us further motivation to be so engaged. We are aware that we easily lose our urgency to share the Good

News and need these extra promptings: a reminder from Jesus to go; and a reminder from God that He has bestowed on us this responsibility, however subject to failure that may seem; and if we have been found, we must invite others to come 'home'.

HOW TO EVANGELIZE

Back to Antioch, and you will recall that the heart of their evangelism appears to have been prayer. It was when they were worshipping and fasting that the Holy Spirit spoke (Acts 13:2), and prayer was the precursor for their sending forth of Barnabas and Paul (13:3). This surely reminds us that the essential prerequisite of evangelism is prayer. Jesus Himself gave clear guidance on this necessity. As He looked out on the situation then (and it is still the same today) and saw the great need for God in the world, His appeal to His disciples was '*Pray!*' They should pray to the Lord of the harvest to send forth reapers (Luke 10:2; Matt. 9:37–38). As we noted in Chapter 4, when the apostle Paul wrote his epistles he included appeals for prayer, including the specific plea, 'Pray for us, too, that God may open a door for our message, so that we may proclaim the mystery of Christ, for which I am in chains. Pray that I may proclaim it clearly, as I should' (Col. 4:3–4). Paul knew the importance of prayer with regard to evangelism, no doubt through his experience at Antioch, but also as he travelled on his missionary journeys.

The praying church at Antioch no doubt included in its prayer requests those individuals for whose souls they had a concern. We know that Jesus prayed personally for Peter, to deliver him from Satan, that his faith might not fail (Luke 22:31–32), and I think we can assume that Lois and Eunice had prayed in the same way for Timothy (2 Tim. 1:5). Although we may pray for a group of people, we need to remember how essential it is to pray for individuals. Often we are discouraged because nothing seems to be changing in the life of the person for whom we are praying, but, conversely, I am sure we have all been encouraged by stories of people who prayed for someone for years but did not live to see the fruit of their prayers, the person being converted after the petitioner's death. Such prayer was indeed answered. So we ought to persevere.

Prayer is an essential prerequisite of evangelism, but when the time or opportunity for words arises, we must speak with gentleness and respect (1 Peter 3:15) and say, 'We have found the Messiah' (John 1:41). We see that the church at Antioch bore much fruit from its willingness to reach out and share the Good News, first in Antioch itself and then, by the sending out of Barnabas and Paul, to other communities in Asia Minor.

We close this chapter with a reminder of the fundamental place of proclamation of the gospel of Jesus Christ by His followers. Paul wrote, 'Woe to me if I do not preach the gospel!'—if I do not tell others about the saving grace of God in Jesus (1 Cor. 9:16).

To think about

» How can we encourage concern for local and worldwide mission within our churches?

» Do you have a longing for a particular person or people to know the Lord? What could you be doing about this?

» How could you support, encourage or be involved in the proclamation of the gospel, whether locally or further afield?

A Holy Spirit-based church

Some of them ... went to Antioch and began to speak to Greeks, telling them the good news about the Lord Jesus. The Lord's hand was with them, and a great number of people believed and turned to the Lord. (Acts 11:20–21)

While they were worshipping the Lord and fasting, the Holy Spirit said, 'Set apart for me Barnabas and Saul for the work to which I have called them.' (13:2)

As we come to examine the next aspect of the church at Antioch I feel as if I am stating the obvious. The church was manifestly guided and indwelt by the Holy Spirit. It could be argued that without His presence and direction it would have no reason to be classified as a Christian church. Many pages have been penned in efforts to fully understand the essence and work of the Holy Spirit, but here, in our consideration of the characteristics of the church at Antioch, our comments will necessarily be basic and introductory.

The Holy Spirit and the birth of the church

We must ask ourselves: Before the events recorded from Acts 11:19, was there a Christian church at Antioch? The answer, surely, must be 'No!' So when did this church come into existence? The Bible text gives us this information. After the martyrdom of Stephen, the Christians living in Jerusalem suffered persecution and were forced to flee the city and live in the surrounding area (Acts 8:1; 11:19). Some of these refugees fled as far north as Antioch, and we see that they were not constricted in any way with regard to speaking about Jesus. Initially, the Good News was shared with only the Jews, but eventually some of the men from Cyprus and Cyrene began with great boldness to preach to Greek inhabitants of the city also, speaking to them of the gospel of Jesus (11:19–20). Preaching

Jesus and His death and resurrection to the Gentiles was not quite an innovation as previously Peter had been led to speak to Cornelius, the Roman centurion (Acts 10). And, just as Peter had seen a positive response to the message, when Cornelius and his household were baptized in the Holy Spirit (10:47–48), so these unnamed evangelists at Antioch saw similar results (11:21). Indeed, in this instance we read that not just a family, a household, turned to the Lord, but 'a great number of people believed' (11:21). Although the Holy Spirit is not mentioned explicitly in this instance, His presence can be inferred from the words 'The Lord's hand was with them'. The Holy Spirit was at work.

Thus the church at Antioch began when the Holy Sprit of God worked in the hearts of those who heard the gospel, the Good News. Viewed in a practical way, the church was formed when there was a body of Christian believers who came together. The church was founded by Christians gathering together for worship and praise. The Holy Spirit in the lives of these new believers was responsible. This contrasts with the modern approach in which, when a new housing estate is built (for example), a church is also built in the hope that some people will wish to attend. In Antioch, what we see is the other way round.

We must remember that initially the church was founded on the Day of Pentecost. On that day the Holy Spirit came and called the listeners to respond to the disciples' message. In other words, He created—gave birth to—Christians who subsequently came together as a 'church' (Acts 2:42). Christian people are Holy Spirit people, and the people at Antioch were obviously Christ's people, gathered to worship. It is interesting to note that on the Day of Pentecost the disciples were already gathered together for worship and prayer, but it was only when the Holy Spirit came upon them that they became a 'church'.

The Holy Spirit and the growth of the church

If the Holy Spirit is responsible for the birth of the church, who is it who makes it grow? Surely it is the same person, the Holy Spirit. This is evidenced at Antioch. We noted that 'the Lord's hand' (surely the Holy Spirit) had used the ministry of those who preached the gospel at Antioch. But we go on to read that the Holy Spirit was responsible for its growth. Working through the ministry of Barnabas (Acts 11:24), the Holy Spirit added further to the number of believers; and through the joint ministry of Barnabas and Paul, many people received Christian teaching. The gathering at Antioch is referred to as a church, and in the community they received the nickname 'Christians' (11:25–26).

Eventually, when it appeared that the church at Antioch was becoming firmly established, we find that it was chosen and called to initiate a new approach to evangelism. It could be said that up to now the Holy Spirit had worked through a scattered people—we have noted that this was how the church at Antioch itself came into being. But now this reliance on itinerant preachers was about to change to a more focused approach. The setting aside and sending out of two members of a congregation, with the express purpose of mission in a set area, was a new venture. But it seems that that decision to venture out on a new missionary project was not purely a church ruling. It wasn't that the church council or elders had met and decided that the time was ripe for missionary expeditions; no, we see that the decision was initiated by the Holy Spirit. Yes, the elders, prophets and teachers were meeting together, worshipping and fasting, when the Holy Spirit expressed His intention in their assembly. In some way He spoke with great clarity to the minds and hearts of those who were gathered, requesting the calling out, and sending out, of Barnabas and Paul (Acts 13:2). These two faithful brothers who had ministered steadfastly at Antioch were to be sent out with the express purpose of preaching the gospel in other areas of that part of the world—and the instigator of this new approach to mission was the Holy Spirit. He spoke, and the church, and Barnabas and Paul, responded in obedience to His direction (13:4).

The Holy Spirit's guidance of individuals in the early church

This is perhaps the clearest illustration in Scripture of the Holy Spirit speaking directly to a church. However, to emphasize the importance of being obedient to the Spirit's instructions, let us remind ourselves of how He gave directions to certain other individuals and the tasks He had for them. After all, even when speaking to the church, His medium was individuals, and ultimately it was individuals who were sent out.

PHILIP

Our first example is the sending of Philip to speak with the eunuch from Ethiopia. Initially, we read that an angel of the Lord was responsible for directing him to the Jerusalem–Gaza road (Acts 8:26). However, once he reached that destination, and the purpose for his presence there was revealed, we note that it was the Holy Spirit who gave Philip directions: 'Go to that chariot and stay near it,' He commands (8:29). Philip counsels the eunuch from the book of Isaiah (Isa. 53:7–8), the eunuch responds in faith to Jesus and is baptized. Philip is then in some way transported to a different place, and we read that it was the Holy Spirit who took him away (8:39). As the eunuch continued his homeward journey, Philip appeared at Azotus, preaching the gospel in that area.

SIMON PETER

While Simon Peter was staying at the house of Simon the tanner at Joppa, three men sent from Cornelius, a centurion living at Caesarea, arrived at the house. Peter had been prepared for their arrival through a dream (Acts 10:9–17), but we read that, when the decisive moment arrived, it was the Holy Spirit who spoke, giving precise instructions to him. As Peter was pondering the vision, the Holy Spirit said, 'Simon, three men are looking for you. So get up and go downstairs. Do not hesitate to go with them, for I have sent them' (10:19–20). Subsequently, following on from Peter's sermon, we read that Cornelius and his household responded positively to his message, received the gift of the Holy Spirit and were baptized (10:47–48). This incident also marked a new venture in the life of the early church: the message being preached to the Gentiles, as was mentioned earlier. Because of some uncertainty concerning these events among the church leadership in Jerusalem, Peter was summoned to offer an explanation (11:1–3). He related all that had happened and was quite clear as to who had authorized and underwritten this venture: 'The Spirit told me to have no hesitation about going with them' (11:12).

This incident is very similar to the concern among the church leaders in Jerusalem regarding the emerging church at Antioch. With regard to the church at Antioch, the leaders sent Barnabas to authenticate the new church (Acts 11:22), but here we see that Peter was being called to account for what he had done (11:1–4). Obviously, in those early days, the church leaders were deeply concerned that each emerging congregation was a genuine work of the Holy Spirit. They were serious about testing the spirits (1 John 4:1). One wonders who would qualify to be such an arbiter today, and what the reaction would be to any negative assessment.

PAUL

Finally, we cannot exit this subject without recollecting the experiences of the apostle Paul with regard to the leading of the Holy Spirit. Perhaps the clearest incident is Paul's experience as he came to the end of his missionary endeavours in Phrygia and Galatia. The question was, where next? Where would God have him carry the Good News now? Initially we see that the message from the Holy Spirit was a negative one: 'kept by the Holy Spirit from preaching the word in the province of Asia …' (Acts 16:6). This was restrictive rather than directive. As most of us no doubt do when one door closes, Paul pushed another. But here once again we see the Holy Spirit imposing a barrier on Paul's probing. He and his companions tried to enter Bithynia, 'but the Spirit of Jesus would not allow them to' (16:7); so they travelled down to Troas, perhaps troubled, bewildered and uncertain where to go next. However, it does not appear that Paul lay awake at night worrying about guidance, for we note that he was sleeping when he saw a vision of a man pleading, 'Come over to Macedonia and help us' (16:9). Paul was convinced that this vision was the Holy Spirit steering him in the direction of Macedonia: 'concluding that God had called us to preach the gospel to them ...' (16:10). So they set off across the Aegean Sea, guided by the Holy Spirit, to proclaim the Good News in Macedonia, arriving first at Neapolis before proceeding to Philippi and an effective ministry—though not without some difficulties accompanying the blessing (16:11–40).

But when it seemed that this itinerant ministry was at an end, where next? To Jerusalem! Paul was convinced that the Holy Spirit was leading him back to Jerusalem, even though he was uncertain what would happen to him there, and although the Holy Spirit had warned him that 'prison and hardships' were awaiting him (20:22–23).

Depending on the Spirit

So the evidence from the church in Antioch is that it was a church that was guided by the Holy Spirit. It was He who directed their work of mission and ministry. We have observed, too, that the early apostles were guided in their Christian activity and outreach by that same Spirit of God. Their projects were initiated and therefore supported and sustained by Him. He was able to bless their endeavours because they were serving in obedience to His call and directing. The enterprises and ventures of the church at Antioch were not based on good ideas or feasible notions (good though these might have been), but on guidance from God. No doubt there are many churches who fall into the trap of becoming 'good idea' fellowships, and end up as activity churches, rather than Spirit-guided churches. We need to remember that 'God's solid foundation stands firm' (2 Tim. 2:19).

This is not to say that God will not lead His church into activity, whether it be proclaiming the Good News by word or deed; indeed, He will. However, it is His leading, rather than our own notions, which is important. Discerning whether an idea for action is personally conceived or God-given is not easy, either. We do know from biblical examples that going it alone rather than waiting for God, and being assured of His leading, can have disastrous effects. The clearest example is that of Moses, who, because of an impulsive action, had to be a shepherd for forty years before being called to lead God's people out of Egypt (Exod. 2:11–3:10). King Saul's disobedience also produced a disastrous outcome: the loss of the throne (1 Sam. 15:1–23)!

The church at Antioch was a Holy Spirit-led church. He it was who worked in their lives (Acts 11:26) and worked through their lives (Acts 13:2). In Chapter 12 we will look more closely at this subject.

To think about

- How can we tell whether a church is led by the Holy Spirit? Does lots of activity necessarily mean a church is full of life?
- Think about your fellowship. Is the Holy Spirit able to work through your activities/ventures/meetings, in lives and through lives?

Chapter 7

A united church

They sailed back to Antioch, where they had been committed to the grace of God for the work they had now completed. On arriving there, they gathered the church together and reported all that God had done through them and how he had opened the door of faith to the Gentiles. And they stayed there a long time with the disciples. (Acts 14:26–28)

When we read the verses relating to the founding of the church at Antioch we can assume there was togetherness. We know from experience that most new ventures start with an overall unity of purpose. It is usually later that divisions occur, as individuals, and possibly even groups, try to assert their authority and to push their ideas to the fore (I recall hearing many years ago that it is in the third generation that enthusiasm wanes and divisions appear).

So by the time the Holy Spirit called forth Barnabas and Paul, we can assume that there was still unity and a bond of peace within this Christian community. This is surely confirmed by the fact that they were meeting together to pray, but even more so by the fact that the Holy Spirit came and spoke to them. Being as He is the basis of unity, the Holy Spirit would not have placed the responsibility of such an important missionary endeavour on a divided and contentious fellowship! The third person of the Trinity would seek out a united community for such a crucial venture. Unity was essential.

As a more concrete example of the unity of the church at Antioch, we can turn to the time when Barnabas and Paul returned from their missionary wanderings. When their missionary travels were over the two evangelists returned to their departure point: to Antioch. There would have been many tales to tell and experiences to relate of what God had achieved through their mission, and it was right that their encounters should be shared with those who had prayed for their journey and ministry. So they returned to Antioch to tell of their adventures in Cyprus, Pamphylia, Iconium, Lystra and Derbe. We read that, when they arrived, 'they gathered the church together' (Acts 14:27). It must have been an exciting meeting, hearing all the news of God's blessing, guidance and protection, and how people had responded to the gospel.

So the church was gathered 'together'—a togetherness which is an essential feature of any church. The church at Antioch was a united church.

The unity of the Godhead

As we seek to learn from Antioch more of this aspect of church life, we are reminded that we worship a united Godhead. The Shema, the creed of the Israelites, declares that 'The LORD our God, the LORD is one' (Deut. 6:4), and although the concept of the Trinity may leave us with a mathematical conundrum, the emphasis of the Scriptures is that God is one. Jesus stresses the union of Himself with the Father: 'I and the Father are one' (John 10:30); and passages such as the following indicate the unity which exists within the Trinity: 'baptising them in the name of the Father and of the Son and of the Holy Spirit' (Matt. 28:19); 'You ... are controlled ... by the Spirit, if the Spirit of God lives in you. And if anyone does not have the Spirit of Christ, he does not belong to Christ' (Rom. 8:9). Particularly in the latter verse, with its interchangeable descriptions of the Spirit, we obtain the impression that the relationships within the Trinity are seamless.

Jesus' desire for unity among his people

It was the deep concern of Jesus that the church should be one. He revealed this concern when speaking about Himself as the good shepherd and referring to His followers as His flock. At the point when He was speaking the flock was incomplete, but He longed to draw in those who were outside the fold, for 'there shall be one flock and one shepherd' (John 10:16). The apostle Paul also expresses this longing when writing to the Ephesian church: 'There is one body and one Spirit ... one hope ... one Lord, one faith, one baptism; one God and Father of all' (Eph. 4:4). Here the predominant word is 'one'. Paul is emphasizing Christ's concern for unity, for oneness.

If it is in the heart of Jesus that His people should live together in unity (Ps. 133:1), we would expect to hear from His lips words which appeal for unity and reveal His longing for accord among His believers. We find this in the oft-quoted words of John's Gospel in what is often referred to as the High Priestly Prayer: 'I pray also for those who will believe in me through their message, that all of them may be one, Father, just as you are in me and I am in you. May they also be in us so that the world may believe that you have sent me' (John 17:20–21); 'May they be brought to complete unity' (17:23). It is the longing of Jesus that all who come to faith in Him, in whatever era or age, may dwell together in unity. This no doubt means unity with their fellow believers—those sharing place and time—but probably also with those who have gone before and those who follow afterwards: a sense of communion with the saints.

The apostles' appeals for unity

If it was the longing and prayer of Jesus that His followers be as one, and enjoy unity and fellowship, it was to be expected that the messages of His apostles would contain the same theme—which of course they do. The apostle Paul is often forthright on this subject, exhorting his readers to unity in more than one letter. In the Epistle to the Romans Paul stresses this longing, instructing his readers to 'Live in harmony with one another' (Rom. 12:16). A further appeal in the same letter is lengthier and comes in the form of a prayer: 'May the God who gives endurance and encouragement give you a spirit of unity among yourselves as you follow

Christ Jesus, so that with one heart and mouth you may glorify the God and Father of our Lord Jesus Christ' (15:5). We will look at this verse again later to see the outcome of the unity for which Paul was pleading. There are similar exhortations to unity in Paul's other letters. Peter expresses the same desire, using similar wording to Paul: 'Finally, all of you, live in harmony with one another' (1 Peter 3:8).

The causes and effects of division

If we are going to seek that unity for which Jesus and His apostles plead, that togetherness which seems to have characterized the church at Antioch, we must remind ourselves of the causes of division and its debilitating effect on Christian living and testimony, to see the damage it does. Division even damaged the relationships of the disciples, Jesus' inner coterie, so let us start there.

DESIRE FOR PRE-EMINENCE

James and John came to Jesus and asked a favour of Him. They wished for the privilege of being seated at either side of Jesus in His glory (Mark 10:37). Jesus, however, was not in a position to grant their request (10:40), but the news of their petition somehow became known to the other disciples and it is recorded that the ten were indignant (10:41). When one considers the volatile nature of Peter in those days, one can imagine that the disciples' reaction may have been fairly strong, and, until Jesus restored calm, relationships would have been strained. On close examination of this incident we can observe the traits displayed by James and John (referred to elsewhere as the Sons of Thunder, Mark 3:17), as well as the inner reactions of the other ten disciples. Desiring a privileged position in heaven may be a commendable yearning, but it depends on the reasons for such a longing. The response of Jesus (as well as of the ten) indicates that perhaps pride and selfish ambition lay behind this request, the wish to be 'top dog'. But that approach created jealousy, anger, mistrust and suspicion in others. Here is a classic formula for division, disunity and possible conflict. This incident is also recorded in the Gospel of Matthew, although in that instance it is the mother of James and John who makes the request on behalf of her sons (Matt. 20:20–28). However, we learn that on another occasion, or possibly on more than one occasion, the disciples argued among themselves as to who would be the greatest. At one time they approached Jesus together to enquire as to who would be the greatest in the kingdom of heaven (Matt. 18:1), to which Jesus responded by calling to him a small child and saying, 'unless you change and become like little children, you will never enter the kingdom of heaven' (Matt. 18:3). In the main, it seems that the disciples were inclined to argue among themselves on the issue, no doubt creating suspicion and division (Mark 9:33–34; Luke 9:46; 22:24).

As well as Jesus using the illustration of a child (Mark 9:36–37; Luke 9:47–48), on occasions He used the concept of servanthood as an indicator of greatness or the 'greatest'. Jesus reminded them that 'If anyone wants to be first, he must be the very last, and the servant of all' (Mark 9:35). One of the disputes on this issue even occurred during the Last Supper (Luke 22:24; how insensitive, we might think! But I have no doubt that many a service of the Lord's Supper has been marred by arrogance and vainglory!). Here again Jesus stresses the notion that greatness is linked with servanthood, and reminds them that one purpose of His presence among them was to serve (Luke 22:26–27).

The desire to occupy the most prominent and important position, even in church circles, is still prevalent in Christian congregations today. As we read of the togetherness of the church at Antioch, perhaps such a desire had not yet infiltrated its gatherings.

THE PERSONALITY CULTURE

As we read Paul's letter to the church at Corinth we discover that that fellowship was being marred by division. Disagreements and quarrels were spoiling the church's unity. The problem was that the congregation was dividing into factions based on the cult of personality. Evidently the different groups of people had been influenced by one or other of these personalities and viewed them as the most important figure in the church, according to their prejudiced opinion (1 Cor. 1:10–12). There was a Paul faction, an Apollos faction, a Cephas faction, and even, for those who were proclaiming deeper piety, a Christ faction. And each group claimed to follow its appointed figurehead, who in some instances may have been the person under whose ministry they had been baptized (1:13). Paul writes to appeal for the divisive attitudes to cease: 'I appeal to you ... that all of you agree with one another so that there may be no divisions among you' (1:10). Such behaviour was inconsistent with Christian commitment and Paul pleaded for it to stop.

Such a personality culture can rear its ugly head even today. It may be in a local congregation, where some members are reluctant to acknowledge the ministry of someone else, preferring to retain an unhelpful allegiance to a favourite former pastor. On a wider scale some are also prejudiced in their regard for certain preachers/teachers. On the international Christian scene we may be aware of influential leaders who, through no fault of their own, are given a celebrity status, and people adopt their favourites. In the church at Corinth the personality culture had created factions, sectarianism, a party spirit, quarrels and ultimately division, just as it does everywhere.

ARROGANCE

Later in the same letter Paul addresses this issue again (1 Cor. 12). Here he is writing in particular about spiritual gifts, but it seems that the reason he is doing so is because even in this area of the church's life division was evident. This passage is, of course, where we have Paul's clear teaching using the 'body' metaphor as the basis of his appeal for unity (12:12–31). Paul stresses the variety of differing personalities, and the variety of gifts and ministries which may be evident in any Christian assembly, and says that it is inevitable that a gathering of people will be diverse; nevertheless, there should be unity, as each one is dependent on the other. There are many causes of division in connection with gifts and ministries, such as self-importance, pomposity, vanity, a superiority complex, elitism and discrimination; all of these had led to an unbearable situation in Corinth, such that Paul had to deal with the issue forcefully and sternly. The basic problem was that some considered their gift superior to others. In this instance Paul commands a preventive, a remedy, as expounded in 1 Corinthians 13: love that is patient, kind, trusting, and so on (1 Cor. 13:4–7). Arrogance about one's own gift creates a selfish, superior attitude which needs to be counteracted by love.

PERSONAL DISAGREEMENTS

For one final example of disunity in the New Testament we turn to Paul's epistle to Philippi. Here the division is highly personalized, and we find Paul naming the culprits: Euodia and Syntyche (Phil. 4:2). Paul does not dwell on their division or its causes, but he pleads with the church, or an individual, to help these two women to reconciliation (4:3). Formerly, they had been united and indeed had shared with Paul in contending for the gospel, but now it seems they were not on speaking terms with one another. Surely now, instead of aiding the cause of the gospel, they were a hindrance to the work and to the effectiveness of the Good News. After all, how can people believe in a Saviour, one who can reconcile man and God, if its adherents are divided? In such circumstances unbelievers are more likely to be repelled than drawn to Christ, and in a sense can be justified in any accusations of hypocrisy against the church. Division of any kind, and the kinds we have considered here, serves to repulse hearers from the message and results in it being ignored. This applies not just to the isolated behaviour of two women, but, as we have seen, to divisions in the whole church as well. No doubt the behaviour of these two women had the potential to divide the church, if people took sides.

In all these examples of division we read an accompanying appeal for unity, stated or implied. However, other appeals are made for unity in the Scriptures, and some of these include notes recording the benefits and blessings of togetherness. It is essential that we remind ourselves of these positive aspects of unity. As one would expect, they are found mainly in Paul's letters.

The benefits of unity

BRINGING GLORY TO GOD

First, in the letter he sent to the church at Rome, Paul follows his plea for unity—'May the God who gives endurance and encouragement give you a spirit of unity among yourselves as you follow Christ Jesus' (Rom. 15:5)—with an explanation of why their unity is necessary and beneficial: 'so that with one heart and mouth you may glorify the God and Father of our Lord Jesus Christ' (15:6). Disunity, then, has a debilitating effect on our worship. Our praise and the glorifying of God are marred.

PEACE

As Paul ends his second letter to Corinth he also implores them to ensure a oneness among themselves. And he again supports his plea with a reminder of the benefit which will ensue from their unity: 'Finally, brothers, goodbye. Aim for perfection, listen to my appeal, be of one mind, live in peace. And the God of love and peace will be with you' (2 Cor. 13:11). Surely Paul is saying that when we live at peace and in unity with each other we will experience an inner contentment. No more suspicions and unease, but the love and peace of God. When we are at ease with God, and at ease with ourselves, we are at ease with others, which consequently enables us to feel as one. 'A heart at peace gives life to the body' (Prov. 14:30).

JOY

Perhaps one of Paul's best-known pleas for unity is found in the letter to the church at Philippi. Here he pleads with the Christians to be 'like-minded, having the same love, being one in spirit and purpose' (Phil. 2:2). If belonging to Christ means anything, he writes, surely it should reveal itself in unity with each other. United with Christ, and in fellowship with the Spirit, equals unity in the assembly of God's people—or it should! And the outcome of this unity for Paul was joy. Unity within the assembly at Philippi would make Paul's joy complete! Surely this effect would be known not only by Paul, but also by others who knew of that church, not least the members of the church themselves.

EFFECTIVE EVANGELISM

Earlier in this letter to the church at Philippi Paul urged the Christians there to conduct themselves 'in a manner worthy of the gospel' (Phil. 1:27a). As we read on we discover that such behaviour is linked with 'contending ... for ... the gospel', which they should do 'in one spirit', 'as one man'. In this way Paul links their conduct with the proclamation of the Good News, with evangelism, implying that effective evangelism is entwined with unity—or, conversely, that evangelism may be hindered by disunity. Written into this verse, then, if not spelled out clearly, is that one of the benefits of unity is effective evangelism. This should be self-evident, as surely division and disagreement just create confusion in the hearts and minds of any hearers. Indeed, sometimes people make even denominationalism, and its appearance of division, an excuse for not heeding the gospel—although in many instances that reaction may be no more than an excuse for rejecting the gospel. So unity enables effectiveness in evangelism, and other benefits include glorifying worship of God, and inner contentment and joy.

Achieving unity

So how does Scripture teach that unity may be achieved? How can assemblies of Christian people be free from division and able to live in unity? The apostle Paul is again the main source of such teaching. First, we go to his letter to the believers in Rome.

HUMILITY AND LOVE

We need to realize that a state of unity is not attained without some discipline and self-denial. Paul pleads with the Christians at Rome to 'Be devoted to one another in brotherly love. Honour one another above yourselves' (Rom. 12:10). We see that, to foster unity in a Christian fellowship, therefore, our attitudes must be affected in two directions: first, towards others, then towards ourselves. Towards others there must be displayed an attitude of devotion and love, and the grace to place others before ourselves, to esteem them above ourselves. This requires true humility and grace. While we must remember that humility is not a condition we can manufacture but something that must flow from the inner presence of God, the path to true humility begins with examining ourselves and discovering what we think of ourselves. It requires a close examination of the ego. Usually we reach the conclusion that we are important and that 'I' am number one—though with the cold assessment of reason we will indeed concede that there are others above us and many below us. But, whatever our standing, or whatever we imagine to be our standing, the scriptural appeal is to honour others above ourselves. This is humility.

Earlier in Romans 12 Paul had already tackled the issue of pride and humility, and had given this remedy: 'Do not think of yourself more highly than you ought, but rather think of yourself with sober judgment, in accordance with the measure of faith God has given you' (12:3). In other words, see yourself as others see you, and, more importantly, as God sees you: as you really are. We have to admit that this is not very easy. As Paul appeals for the Roman church to live in harmony, he adds, 'Do not be proud, but be willing to associate with people of low position' (12:15). Living in accordance with such teaching should, by the grace of God, produce unity.

When we turn to Paul's epistle to the church at Philippi we find that he adopts a similar approach to the matter of unity. The first five verses of Philippians 2 are well known among Bible-reading Christians, and are almost as notable as the subsequent six verses. We considered the first two verses of this chapter above, regarding the benefits of unity. Now Paul turns to guiding them on the path to unity: 'Do nothing out of selfish ambition or vain conceit, but in humility consider others better than yourselves. Each of you should look not only to your own interests, but also to the interests of others' (Phil. 2:3–4). He then adds, 'Be like Jesus' (see 2:5). Here again is the plea to put others, and their interests, at least on a par with our own. Consider them better than yourselves, he says—an instruction which clearly requires self-denial and humility. Attaining unity among Christians is clearly not easy to achieve—indeed, it is impossible unless all are seeking a united relationship, because otherwise someone who is following Paul's teaching diligently may be taken advantage of and possibly discouraged. All have to be seeking unity for it to be attained.

Peter also, in his first epistle, makes a similar plea for unity, adding advice as to how harmony and unity may be reached (1 Peter 3:8–9). Peter's instruction has the same two elements as Paul's: an attitude to others and an understanding of oneself. With regard to our relationship with one another, he pleads for compassion, sympathy and love, having a brotherly concern. Regarding oneself, he again advocates humility. Peter also adds that we be not vindictive or vengeful towards anyone who insults us, abuses us or hurts us, but respond with a blessing.

FORGIVENESS

For our final example of advice on godly living which ought to lead to harmonious relationships within the Christian fellowship, we turn back to the apostle Paul, and his instructions to the church at Colossae. Paul tells the church there that they are called to live at peace with one another (3:15), but in the preceding verses he gives his guidelines. First, he calls for holy living. He urges them to have compassion, kindness, gentleness, humility and patience (Col. 3:12), and then he encourages them to bear with each other and forgive each other (3:13). Forgiveness is, of course, a basic tenet of the gospel. The clearest example in the teaching of Jesus is when He reminded Peter of how often he ought to forgive: seventy-seven times (Matt. 18:21–22)! He then told the parable of the unmerciful servant to illustrate His point. As Paul reminds his readers, God has indeed forgiven us through the death of Christ on the cross (Col. 2:13), a condition which Paul uses to encourage us to be forgiving. And Paul's final appeal, like that of Peter, is for love which creates unity (Col. 3:14), covers over a multitude of sins (1 Peter 4:8) and fulfils the law (Rom. 13:8).

There are other verses which we could consider with regard to unity, but we close this section with one quote from the book of Psalms: 'How good and pleasant it is when brothers live together in unity!' (Ps. 133:1).

The church at Antioch is a church that is in harmony, a church with unison, a togetherness (Acts 14:27); and as we prepare to spend time in the presence of the Christians there, may we appreciate the blessings of unity and assimilate a desire to foster harmony in our own fellowships: a togetherness in prayer, in worship, in service, in witness, in fellowship, in encouraging, in sympathy, in empathy; a togetherness in the Lord.

Let us take on board these words of the apostle Paul as he closes his letter to the church in Rome: 'I urge you, brothers, to watch out for those who cause divisions and put obstacles in your way that are contrary to the teaching you have learned. Keep away from them' (Rom. 16:17).

To think about

- Think about your church. To what extent would you describe it as 'united'? What can you do to encourage unity, and discourage disunity?
- Look again at the verses we have considered in this chapter: Romans 12:3, 10; Philippians 2:3; 1 Peter 3:8–9; Colossians 3:12–15. Reflect upon or discuss how the teaching in these verses should be put into practice.

A giving church

During this time, some prophets came down from Jerusalem to Antioch. One of them, named Agabus, stood up and through the Spirit predicted that a severe famine would spread over the entire Roman world ... The disciples, each according to his ability, decided to provide help for the brothers living in Jerusalem. This they did, sending their gift to the elders by Barnabas and Saul. (Acts 11:27–30)

The subject of giving is usually a very sensitive matter, even in Christian circles. Someone has said that when we come to Christ, the last part of our lives to be converted is our purse or wallet. Perhaps, like me, you have been present in a gathering where the subject of giving has been raised and you have experienced the heated reactions it has provoked. Tithing, in particular—even the mention of it—can create an adverse reaction. Sometimes the debate as to whether one calculates the tithe before or after tax is used as a delaying tactic!

Sadly, some churches strengthen the opinions of outsiders that the church is always asking for money. Fairs and rummage sales, which for some congregations seem to be the main source of fundraising, are usually well advertised and offer justification to those who hold this view. On the other hand, I recall a preacher once saying that he was often accused of always preaching about money, when in reality he could not remember when he had last done so. In other words, in the minds of some people there exists a prejudice against churches on this issue. But it is not wrong to preach on the biblical approach to giving—it is a genuine subject within the Scriptures.

It is sad that the world perceives this image of the church and of God. This is because, in one sense, God does not need anyone's money or financial aid. After all, the cattle on a thousand hills are His (Ps. 50:10), and He feeds the birds of the air and clothes the fields (Matt. 6:26, 30), so what need has He of anyone's wealth? Indeed, God has Himself through Christ paid the price of our salvation (1 Cor. 6:20; 7:23); we are saved by grace, by the gift of God (Eph. 2:8). This does not in any way cancel out the Christian responsibility financially to support the Lord's work of extending His kingdom. It only challenges us to ensure that those outside the kingdom do not receive the wrong impression.

As we continue our visit to the church at Antioch, we find that, along with its other attributes, it is a giving church. While, in the early days of the church, Barnabas and Paul were busy teaching and preaching, some prophets came from Jerusalem (Acts 11:27). This was a very exciting time for the church at Antioch—a time of church growth and spiritual understanding (11:24–26)—but into the situation came these visitors from Jerusalem with disturbing news. One of the visitors, Agabus, 'predicted that a severe famine would spread over the entire Roman world' (11:28), a prophecy which came true. How would the Christians at Antioch respond?

Well, just as the churches in Macedonia and Achaia responded to the needs of the church in Jerusalem (Rom. 15:25–27; 2 Cor. 8:1–4; 9:2) and the church at Philippi responded to the needs of Paul (Phil. 4:14–15), so the church at Antioch responded by giving generously for the coming emergency (Acts 11:29). Just as they were able (1 Cor. 16:2), the Christians gave donations to the fund to meet the expected shortfall. This church may have been a young church, and may even have had some of the expenses that emerging churches have, but they gave generously to the churches in Judea, and entrusted funds into the care of Barnabas and Paul for safe delivery (Acts 11:30).

Our generous God

PROVISION FOR ALL MANKIND

As we ponder on the generosity of the Antioch church, let us remind ourselves of God's liberality, His giving. In complete contrast to the world's search for wealth and material possessions, God is a generous, giving God. This generosity is revealed in the very first chapter of the Bible. As we come to the end of the details of the creation which took place on that sixth day—livestock, animals and, ultimately, man—we see that God offered the fruit of creation for man's benefit: 'I give you every seed-bearing plant on the face of the whole earth and every tree that has fruit with seed in it. They will be yours for food' (Gen. 1:29). This provision of sustenance was not limited to man either, for we read that 'to all the beasts of the earth and all the birds of the air and all the creatures that move on the ground—everything that has the breath of life in it—I give every green plant for food' (1:30).

After the destruction of the earth from the flood, God spoke to His servant Noah and extended even further the range of His provision for mankind: 'Everything that lives and moves will be food for you [beasts, birds and fish]. Just as I gave you the green plants, I now give you everything' (9:3). Such generosity: everything! The fact that some of us in the world, for various reasons—often greed and selfishness—do not have enough food to sustain life does not take anything away from the reality that God has given us the fruit of the earth as our food. It is not His fault that there is want; it is our injustice that is the problem.

GIFTS FOR HIS PEOPLE

The gift of the fruit of the earth for food is of a general nature: it is for the benefit of the whole of God's creation. However, we are also aware that God gives gifts of a particular nature. This is evidenced in particular subsequent to the call and election of His chosen people, Israel. God made a specific offer to His people. As Abraham stood on the higher ground between Bethel and Ai, God came and spoke to him, and encouraged him to look around, to the north, south, east and west. As he gazed about, viewing the surrounding landscape, the Lord said, 'All the land that you see I will give to you and your offspring for ever' (Gen. 13:15). After promising him a large family of offspring (13:16), God reiterates His promise of a land: 'walk through the length and breadth of the land, for I am giving it to you' (13:17). Though at a later date, when speaking to Moses, God reminded the people of their responsibilities in the land, and also that they were but tenants (Lev. 25:23), it was rent-free, a gift. It was a land for His people in which they would dwell.

When we turn to the New Testament, we discover further evidence of the generosity of God. It is of course a gift from God on which the Christian faith is based: the gift of His only begotten Son, Jesus. This is an example of pure sacrificial giving. In the words of perhaps the best-known verse in the Bible, 'God so loved the world that he *gave* his one and only Son, that whoever believes in him shall not perish but have eternal life' (John 3:16, emphasis added). Not only was it a sacrificial gift, but we read that the gift of God's Son was motivated by love, so that we might receive eternal life through faith. To say that Jesus is a gift from God does not fully reveal the implications of such a gift. Even to say that this was the supreme illustration of an act of sacrificial giving does not totally reveal the cost. Perhaps it is only when we recognize and acknowledge our sinful depravity, and its consequences, that the full depth of the love that lies behind such an act is revealed. It is a love that brings redemption from the consequences of sin, deliverance from death and hope of eternal life, but achieved at such a tremendous cost: the scourging and crucifixion of the Son of God. The gift from God of His Son is life to those who believe, but the opposite to those who refuse, which is tantamount to the rejection of God's gift. Paul, writing to the church in Rome, states that 'the wages of sin is death', but he stresses that 'the gift of God is eternal life in Christ Jesus our Lord' (Rom. 6:23). And writing to the Christians in Ephesus, Paul reminds them that salvation, by grace through faith, is not something we can achieve ourselves; it is the gift of God (Eph. 2:8). Deliverance from death, the consequence of our own sinfulness, is offered to us as a gift from God.

We see a further example of the generosity of God and His liberality in giving on the Day of Pentecost. As Peter stood preaching in Jerusalem, giving the first evangelistic sermon, he informed the people of, among other matters, a further gift from God. After calling them to repentance and baptism, to know the forgiveness of sin through Jesus, Peter stated that yielding to Christ in this way would result in their receiving the Holy Spirit (Acts 2:38)—the Spirit who was promised in the context of the coming of a new covenant (Jer. 31:31–34; Isa. 44:3; Joel 2:29). This, in a way, was the promise of the gift of His very presence, affirming the genuineness of our repentance and faith, guaranteeing our hope of eternity (Eph. 1:13–14) and enabling us to live a life of love and effectiveness for Him (Gal. 5:22–23; 1 Cor. 12:7–11). It was also a fulfilment of Jesus' promise to be with us always (Matt. 28:20). These are but a few examples demonstrating that the only God, who revealed Himself to Abraham, Isaac and Jacob, and sent His Son, Jesus, into the world, is a generous, giving God.

Giving as our response to God

Although God does not need anything from us, He does look for an expression of gratitude, a response in thanksgiving. When the children of Israel became settled in the Promised Land, the land God had given them, Moses instructed them that, as a mark of thanksgiving, they should take the firstfruits of their toil and present them to the Lord (Deut. 26:1–11). As well as being a reminder that what they now had, and where they now resided, was a gift from God, this offering also carried with it an expression of gratitude to Him. Earlier in his closing address to the people Moses had reminded them of the amount which was to be the total of their offering: a tithe. These tithes had to be taken every three years to the appointed towns (Deut. 14:28). Moses here gives three reasons for the ingathering: so that the Levites could be provided for (the Levites were not allowed to own land); so that the aliens, widows and orphans could eat and be satisfied; and 'so that the LORD your God may bless you in all the work of your hands' (14:29). From a negative point of view, Malachi declares in his prophecy that failure to bring in the tithes and offerings is tantamount to robbing God (Mal. 3:8–9), and he continues by pleading, on God's behalf, that they bring the full tithe into the storehouse (3:10); if they do so, God will pour out blessing upon them (3:10–12).

As we noted at the beginning of this chapter, the giving of the church at Antioch was in response to a need that was presented to them. Perhaps this giving was not in the manner prescribed in the Old Testament (after all, it was a Gentile church), but we know that they gave generously towards the needs of the church in Judea (Acts 11:29).

How should we give?

This brings us to consider for ourselves: how do we give? What should be our attitude to giving and being generous? Paul, in his two letters to the church at Corinth, gives us the clearest instruction on this subject, so it is to these letters that we chiefly refer.

WILLINGLY, ACCORDING TO OUR ABILITY

How should we give? One sensible answer to that question is that we cannot give what we do not have. In other words, the expectation of God is that we give from what we have. Paul makes this point as he writes to the Corinthian church: 'if the willingness is there, the gift is acceptable according to what one has, not according to what he does not have' (2 Cor. 8:12). With regard to the church at Antioch and their gift to the church in Judea, they gave 'each according to his ability' (Acts 11:29), and there is a clear implication in this verse that they gave willingly.

These principles of willingness and giving from what we have are found in the Old Testament also. When materials were being gathered for the building of the tabernacle, Moses took the same approach as Paul: 'From what you have,' said Moses, 'take an offering for the LORD. Everyone who is willing is to bring ...' (Exod. 35:5). Towards the end of the chapter we read that all 'who were willing brought to the LORD freewill offerings' (35:29). This overt generosity led to a mildly embarrassing situation in which Moses had to restrain the people from giving more because the donations exceeded the need (36:6–7).

THOUGHTFULLY

In two further instances Paul takes up the same theme when writing to the church in Corinth. Paul again says that giving should be exercised willingly—'not reluctantly or under compulsion, for God loves a cheerful giver' (2 Cor. 9:7)—and also that they should not give arbitrarily, but in a predetermined way: 'Each man should give what he has decided in his heart to give' (2 Cor. 9:7); 'set aside a sum of money in keeping with his income' (1 Cor. 16:2). Note the emphasis on giving from what you have: 'in keeping with his income'; and on giving willingly: 'God loves a cheerful giver.'

FROM A COMMITMENT TO GOD AND OUR FELLOW BELIEVERS

Two further aspects of giving which Paul propounds relate specifically to self and God. In his second letter to the Corinthians Paul holds up the Macedonian churches as a challenging example (2 Cor. 8:4). Certainly we see that they were a church eager to give to meet the needs of others. It is evident that the Christians at Macedonia were under extreme difficulties, including poverty, yet we read that their hearts overflowed with joy and generosity. Without compunction, without any pressure, they gave 'beyond their ability', counting it a privilege to contribute to the needs of the saints in a clear display of selflessness (8:3–4). The impetus to give came from their commitment to God: 'they gave themselves first to the Lord' (8:5); and we read that they were also committed to their fellow believers and the Christian ministry: 'and then to us'.

TO BRING PRAISE TO GOD, NOT ONESELF

Another aspect of giving is that it should be done, not to receive praise for oneself or to impress others with one's own largesse, but to bring praise to God. Giving is not only for the meeting of the needs of others, but that there may be an overflowing of 'expressions of thanks to God' (2 Cor. 9:12–13). Paul illustrates this point as he writes with thankfulness to the church at Philippi. He states that it was not only their gift which was noteworthy, but also what it indicated about the condition of their hearts before the Lord (Phil. 4:17).

The generosity of the Macedonian Christians revealed that their hearts were right with God: 'they gave themselves first to the Lord'. The generosity of the Philippian Christians revealed that they too had hearts in tune with God. Of the Christians at Antioch we read that they were encouraged to 'remain true to the Lord with all their hearts' (Acts 11:23), so we can justifiably presume that their giving was an indicator of this fact. If we are to learn anything about giving from the church at Antioch, it is that giving begins with a heart that is given to the Lord. It is for this reason that I have not examined any practical questions such as how much we should give, nor even stressed the matter of tithing, but have concentrated on the attitude of the heart. Giving should be our response to a generous God; it is an expression of our thankfulness and our praise to Him.

To think about

» Look again at the following verses we considered in this chapter: 1 Corinthians 16:2; 2 Corinthians 8:4–5, 12; 9:7, 12–13. Reflect further on the question, 'How ought we to give?'

» What is your own attitude to giving, and how does it compare with the attitude of the Christians in Macedonia, Philippi and Antioch?

Chapter 9

A hospitable church

So for a whole year Barnabas and Saul met with the whole church and taught great numbers of people. (Acts 11:26)

And they stayed there a long time with the disciples. (14:28)

As we continue to walk through the streets of Antioch, heading towards the church there, perhaps you feel a sense of nervousness and hesitancy as you wonder about the reception we will receive. Will we receive a warm, open-hearted welcome? Will this be a hospitable church?

Thus far, the characteristics of the church at Antioch have been revealed in the Scriptures in a fairly obvious way. There are quite clear statements which manifest openly that the church is soundly taught, is well fed, and is a worshipping, praying, witnessing and giving fellowship—but what about it being an accessible, receptive church?

Evidence in this area may not be obvious, but it can be observed just below the surface. And it can emerge into the open by posing the simple question: Where did Barnabas and Paul reside? Where did these two visiting teachers stay? The answer must surely be: with the disciples in the city of Antioch. You will recall that their visits were not just short-term sojourns; they were not passing through on their way to somewhere else. As we have seen, Barnabas arrived first. We do not know how long this initial period lasted, but we do know that, after he had been to Tarsus and returned with Paul, who was to share in the ministry, together they stayed for a whole year meeting with the church and teaching great numbers of people (Acts 11:26). Later, when Barnabas and Paul returned from their missionary journey, they gathered together the church to submit their report, and then remained there a long time with the disciples (Acts 14:27–28). Someone, or perhaps more than one person, was willing to open their home and offer hospitality to these visiting preachers, who appeared to be there for an indeterminate length of time.

In the third letter of John we note that the apostle commends his dear friend Gaius for the hospitality he has offered to Christian travellers passing through the town where he lived, suggesting that to do so is a Christian responsibility (3 John 1–8). However, not everyone is enthusiastic about being involved in this ministry.

Definition of hospitality

What is 'hospitality'? 'Hospitality', 'hospital' and even 'hostel' have the same root and similar meaning, and the latter two give us a clear indication in this respect. Derived from the Latin, 'hospitality' simply means to receive guests, including the sick and the elderly. This kind of caring was a ministry exercised by some monasteries, which often included a hospital among their buildings. The word also means welcoming and being generous to guests, and being kind to strangers. The Greek word *philoxenia*, translated 'hospitable', is more explicit in that literally it means 'love of strangers'. Indeed, in the letter to the Hebrews the word is translated 'entertain strangers' (Heb. 13:2). This verse particularly resonates with the teaching of Jesus. When He was invited to dine at the home of a prominent Pharisee (Luke 14:1), after making comments on the fact that some of the guests were clamouring to sit in the honoured places at the table, and reminding them of the possibility of humiliation if subsequently they were asked to move lower (Luke 14:8–11; cf. Prov. 25:6–7), Jesus gave advice on whom to invite for luncheon/dinner (Luke 14:12):

do not invite your friends, your brothers or relatives, or your rich neighbours; if you do, they may invite you back, and so you will be repaid. But when you give a banquet, invite the poor, the crippled, the lame, the blind, and you will be blessed. Although they cannot repay you, you will be repaid at the resurrection of the righteous. (Luke 14:12–14)

Surely this is a most challenging and radical way of extending hospitality! The guests usually invited to a meal, particularly a banquet, would be family and very close friends; not anyone who was unknown, especially the sorts of people Jesus was advocating: the poor, the lame—those on the fringes of society. However, when we look at the meanings of the word 'hospitality', these are the very people to whom we should be extending invitations to dine. Perhaps we do not normally ask people for a meal in the expectancy that they will return the favour, although that could be the outcome. Here, though, the guiding principle seems to be to invite those who are *unable* to return the favour—at least on some occasions!

This most challenging aspect of hospitality will cause much heart-searching. However, as well as strangers to whom we could offer meals, there will also be those known to us who, because of their situation, are in need of hospitality. It is necessary to minister to them in a hospitable way too, for in doing so we may be ministering to a needy situation as well as showing a caring spirit. I am sure that under this heading we can include our friends, as this is a valuable way of encouraging our unity in Christ and strengthening our fellowship; and we can include family too, as we show our care for them. I am sure Jesus enjoyed such hospitality with His friends in the home of Martha, Mary and Lazarus (Luke 10:38–42). Also, such action is a way in which we 'do good to … those who belong to the family of believers' (Gal. 6:10). Perhaps inviting people we know is the easiest way of offering hospitality. But, in the light of what we have been considering, we should not be hesitant about doing this, nor feel guilty, as surely it is an essential ministry and one which not everyone is gifted to fulfil; and, of course, some, in receipt of such benevolence, will not be able to reciprocate.

Biblical examples of hospitality

We can find many examples of hospitality in the Scriptures.

ABRAHAM

As Abraham sat at the entrance of his tent near the great trees of Mamre (Gen. 18:1), he suddenly became conscious of three men standing nearby, whom he invited into his dwelling for refreshment and food. He fed them quite a banquet: curds, milk and a calf (18:3–8). This is a good example of offering hospitality to strangers and, in so doing, entertaining angels unawares (Heb. 13:2), as these visitors, after they had eaten, went on to proclaim that Sarah, who was old and past child-bearing, would, in a year's time, give birth to a son (18:10–11).

RAHAB

Another illustration can be found in someone who was not a member of the family of God but an inhabitant of Jericho, and a prostitute at that: Rahab (Josh. 2:1). Jericho was the first city which would have to be conquered by the people of Israel as they entered the land of Canaan. However, before they crossed the river Jordan, Joshua sent two spies to check out the lie of the land, and it was these two men who were offered hospitality by Rahab. These men were not just strangers, but were indeed enemy spies. However, Rahab recognized that, as representatives of Israel, these two men were truly envoys of God, and this fact was her motivation in being willing to offer them protection (2:9–12). For this act of kindness Rahab subsequently received her reward—not just the one she will receive at the future resurrection of the righteous (Luke 14:13–14), but almost immediately, because at the eventual destruction of Jericho only Rahab and her family were saved (Josh. 6:17, 22–23, 25). Rahab's name appears on the list of people of faith in the letter to the Hebrews, where her salvation during the desolation and massacre of Jericho is attributed to her faith which led her to offer hospitality (Heb. 11:31).

THE WIDOW OF ZAREPHATH

Elijah and Elisha both benefited from the generosity of two open-hearted women who were willing to open their homes. After Elijah prophesied that there was to be a drought in Israel, he was led by the Lord to the brook Kerith, where he was fed by ravens (1 Kings 17:1–6). When the brook ran dry, the word of the Lord came again to Elijah, this time directing him to Zarephath of Sidon, and to the home of a widow who dwelt there (17:7–10). How the Lord provided food for Elijah, the widow and her son, and how the Lord used Elijah in the miraculous raising of the boy from death are other aspects of this story (17:12–24), but the main lesson from this incident for us now is that the widow opened her home to the prophet, and food was provided for them in a season of great dearth (17:15). It could be said that in this situation the woman received food and the restoration to life of her son because she had opened the door of her home and offered hospitality to a stranger—Elijah. We note also that Elijah's stay in Zarephath was not short, but approached three years (18:1).

THE SHUNAMMITE WOMAN

Elisha had a not dissimilar experience with a Shunammite woman, who offered him hospitality in her home. This does not seem to have been on a permanent basis; rather, she prepared a room for him and offered him a meal whenever he was in the area (2 Kings 4:8–10). This was a haven for Elisha on his journeys, a place where he found rest and refreshment (4:11). And, as seems usual, there was blessing for the one who extended the warm welcome: the Shunammite woman. In this instance, however, the ensuing events might seem bewildering. First, the woman, who was childless, was granted a son (4:14–17), but in a twist to this tale, when he was a young boy, he died (4:20). The Shunammite summoned Elisha, and, through his prayerful and dramatic intervention, her son was raised to life again (4:32–35).

Without delving into the theological backgrounds of these events, but remaining with the practical, surface elements, we note that each of the examples of hospitality we have considered here was accompanied by a miraculous blessing. As we have seen, these miracles were often centred around children: births to women who were too old, and/or those offspring being raised from the dead.

MARTHA AND MARY

Although the first example of hospitality we are about to consider from the New Testament is not accompanied by an unexpected birth, it is nevertheless linked by a raising from the grave. For this example we go to Bethany, to the home of Martha and Mary. The incident in the Gospels, recorded by Luke, concentrates on the minor dispute between the two sisters (Luke 10:38–42). Martha is grieved that Mary is not giving any help in the kitchen towards the preparation of the meal, preferring to sit at the feet of Jesus, and no doubt learning from Him. Here we simply note that these two women had opened their home to Jesus and His disciples. They offered Jesus hospitality, probably on more than one occasion, and their home was a place where He was able to rest and be refreshed, a place where He always found a welcome (Luke 10:38–42). Perhaps Jesus' full appreciation of this home and His affection for its owners is revealed when He is informed of the death of Martha and Mary's brother, Lazarus. As Jesus went to this house in Bethany to visit the grieving sisters we read that He was moved in spirit and troubled. We are also told, 'Jesus wept' (John 11:35). The outcome was that, just as the sons of the widow of Zarephath and the Shunammite woman had been restored to life, so was Lazarus (John 11:43–44).

THE UPPER ROOM

A further example of hospitality offered to Jesus was the Upper Room. It was here that Jesus met with His disciples for their final meal together, the Last Supper (Luke 22:7–12 etc.). It was obviously in the home of someone who made Jesus welcome and who was willing to make a room available for Him. There is a clear indication that the room had already been prepared for Jesus to celebrate the Passover with His disciples (Luke 22:11–12).

Not only was this room available for Jesus to use it to meet with His friends and companions, but, after the death of Jesus, it seems likely that it was also available as a meeting point for His followers. After the ascension of Jesus, the disciples 'went upstairs to the room where they were staying' (Acts 1:13). This was a place where they met for prayer (1:14), and it is possible that it was in this same room that the disciples were gathered on the Day of Pentecost when they were anointed with the Holy Spirit (2:1–4). This may also have been the house to which Peter returned after his amazing escape from prison (12:7–10), a house where the disciples were gathered to pray for his release and which is identified as being the home of Mary the mother of John Mark (7:12). If so, this Mary, together with the other Mary and her sister Martha, is an outstanding example of generous hospitality—not only to Jesus, but to his disciples as well. We can only speculate as to the size of John Mark's mother's home when we read of how many were present following Jesus' ascension: all the disciples, Jesus' brothers and His mother, and some more of His female followers. Was the room large enough to accommodate 120 people (Acts 1:15)?

SIMON THE TANNER AND CORNELIUS

I have no doubt that as Peter and the other disciples fulfilled their itinerant ministry, going from place to place, they benefited from hospitality and were gladly welcomed into people's homes. One such incident in Peter's life occurred at Joppa. Following the raising back to life of Tabitha (Dorcas), Peter stayed at the home of Simon, a tanner (Acts 9:36–43). He stayed there 'for some time', and indeed he was still residing at Joppa when three members of the household of the centurion Cornelius came to ask him to go to Caesarea (10:1–23). The outcome of that visit to Cornelius was, as we know, that he and his family came to faith in Jesus: the first recorded Gentile converts (10:44–46). Subsequent to this experience we find that once again Peter was offered hospitality in someone's home—that of Cornelius (10:48). As a result of Peter's preaching, Cornelius and his household had been brought to faith, and the immediate response of the centurion was to offer Peter hospitality. We see the same response to conversion in our next example, in the life of the apostle Paul.

LYDIA

Having been led to Philippi by the vision of the man of Macedonia (Acts 16:6–10), Paul, Silas and Luke went down to the riverside in search of a place of prayer, and while there began to speak to some of the women who were gathered (16:13). It is said of one of the women, Lydia, that the 'Lord opened her heart to respond to Paul's message', and consequently she and her household were baptized (16:14–15). What was Lydia's response? '"If you consider me a believer in the Lord," she said, "come and stay at my house"' (16:15). This was a firm offer of hospitality.

AQUILA AND PRISCILLA

We also know that Paul enjoyed hospitality in the home of Aquila and Priscilla (Acts 18:3). This was at their home in Corinth. They had just arrived there from Rome, from where they, and all the Jews, had been expelled by the emperor Claudius (18:2). Paul, newly arrived from Athens, lived with this dear Christian couple for some time (18:18). Aquila and Priscilla were tentmakers, as was Paul, so he joined with them in their business (18:3). It is possible that through the shared trade Paul made some contribution to his upkeep (see 1 Thes. 2:9; 2 Thes. 3:8). However, we must not let that detract from the fact that Aquila and

Priscilla welcomed Paul into their home. This was not an isolated example of hospitality on their part as, following a subsequent move to Ephesus, they there invited Apollos into their home (18:24–26). It seems that this godly pair were willing to open their home to their fellow believers wherever they dwelt.

GOVERNOR PUBLIUS

When Paul was being taken as a prisoner to Rome to appeal to Caesar (Acts 25:11; 28:19) he suffered shipwreck off the coast of Malta, to which everyone on board was washed ashore (27:44). Paul there had a miraculous encounter with a snake (its venom had no ill effect on him and he shook it off into the fire, 28:3–6). After this, Paul and members of his entourage were welcomed into the home of the governor, Publius, where for three days they were treated hospitably (28:7). Again we note that there was a pleasing consequence to this willingness of someone to open their home to others: the governor's father was sick of a fever and dysentery, but following prayerful ministry by Paul he was made well (28:8).

When Paul arrived in Rome, it is possible that he stayed in the home of one of the believers (28:23) before renting a home of his own (28:30), where, no doubt, he stayed during his house arrest.

The rewards of showing hospitality

At this point we must pause to reflect on the consequences of hospitality. As noted in the examples above, the offering of hospitality is often accompanied by a blessing. This may cause us to think that if we offer hospitality, we will receive a reward. While it may be the case that, as a result of offering hospitality, some blessing will follow, that blessing will not necessarily be of a tangible nature. However, as we learn from the parable of the sheep and the goats, if hospitality is offered with a sincere heart, it will lead to sharing in the inheritance from the Lord (Matt. 25:34–36).

Who should offer hospitality?

It seems that offering hospitality is a gift, yet it is a gift which is not exclusive to a few. In his letter to the church at Rome Paul states quite clearly and simply, 'Practise hospitality' (Rom. 12:13), an appeal which is addressed to the church, not individuals. Peter, in his first letter, makes a similar general request: 'Offer hospitality to one another' (1 Peter 4:9). We have noted how John encouraged the offering of hospitality to itinerant Christian preachers (3 John 8). In his Pastoral Letters Paul lists hospitality as one of the attributes required of those being considered for the posts of overseer (1 Tim. 3:2: 'self-controlled, respectable, hospitable') and elder (Titus 1:8: 'he must be hospitable'). Also, in his letter to Timothy, Paul stresses that for a widow to be included on the list for 'benefits', not only must she be over sixty, but she must also, among other qualifications, have shown hospitality, presumably when she was in a position to do so (1 Tim. 5:10).

Hospitality extends beyond offering food (and/or board and lodging); it goes beyond simply opening one's home, because it involves having a heart open towards others and their needs. It is possible that one is an indication of the other. A guide on the matter is found when Jesus sent out the twelve disciples, in twos, to carry the gospel to the surrounding villages (Matt. 10:9–14; Mark 6:8–11; Luke 9:3–5). Jesus told them that, when they approached a house, if they were made welcome they were to stay there, but if they were not well received they were to depart, leave the town, and shake its dust from off their feet. The implication was that if the residents of a village were unwilling to open their homes to the disciples, they would not open their hearts to the gospel.

As we approach the church at Antioch, having been reminded of what it means to be hospitable, we know that this church is so inclined and that we will be welcomed warmly in their fellowship. It is a hospitable church: they opened their homes to the disciples, they opened their hearts to the gospel and they opened their church to strangers.

To think about

- » What might hinder us from showing hospitality and opening our homes to others?
- » Consider how, in your situation, whether as an individual, a group or a family, you can offer hospitality to others.

A maturing church

News of this reached the ears of the church at Jerusalem, and they sent Barnabas to Antioch ... Then Barnabas went to Tarsus to look for Saul, and when he found him, he brought him to Antioch. So for a whole year Barnabas and Saul met with the church and taught great numbers of people. (Acts 11:22, 25–26)

As we visit this church in Antioch we ask ourselves: How long has it been in existence? We can presume that by the time news of its creation reached Jerusalem (Acts 11:22) it had been established for a year at the most. That was when the elders decided to send Barnabas to confirm the authenticity of the faith of that gathering. We also know that Barnabas, together with Paul, remained in Antioch for at least a year, teaching the members of the fellowship (11:26).

An associated question is: What would be the spiritual age of its members? When we read of them in Acts 11, how long had they been Christians? Well, surely that would be similar to the length of existence of the church: a year or two! In other words, they would have been young in the faith—yet I think we see in them a maturity beyond their spiritual age. I suggest that we are going to visit a church that is growing not just numerically, but also in Christian understanding. And not just in biblical knowledge either, but also in its practical outworking. The members of the church at Antioch were probably much younger in the faith than some of us, but we see in them an amazing maturity. Neither do I consider this to be a static condition, but an ongoing state—that is, it is a *maturing* church, rather than a mature, fully grown community.

Maturing, not mature

Many fellowships today fall into the trap of considering that they have 'arrived'. Some may deny that they have such an attitude, but their manner and disposition belie their claims. Often the impression they give of superiority conveys that inwardly this is how they consider themselves. The comments some folk make about their fellowship often convey the same impression. The expression 'sheep-stealing' indicates this reality: 'Join us—our fellowship is better than ...' Sadly, unbeknown to those who make these claims, this is a sign of immaturity and of a need for growth. And who among us dare not include themselves in this category? However, it seems that the church at Antioch had no such pretensions and as a result was reaching forwards, striving for maturity.

As we shall consider shortly, the Christian life is mirrored in human life: that is, we are born and then we grow, hopefully into maturity. Similarly, the above-mentioned attitude of self-satisfaction can also be seen at a human level. Even in old age, it reveals a lack of wisdom if we consider that we know everything. We may think we have greater understanding with age than we did when we were young, and this ought to be true, yet it is unwise to think we know everything—sadly, sometimes we have the temerity to give the impression that we do. This is an attitude which can cause resentment in others, particularly the young. Sometimes the wisdom of age reveals how little we really do know.

Christian faith has a beginning, whether this birth is sudden and spontaneous, as with Paul on the way to Damascus, or is a slower process of gradual understanding and enlightenment. It could be argued that the disciples took three years to come to faith! So as Christians we are born—born again, as the Scriptures tell us (1 Peter 1:23; John 1:12–13; 3:3). And just as where there is physical birth there ought to be physical growth—growth in character, mental understanding and hopefully wisdom—so if there is spiritual birth there should be accompanying spiritual growth. We read in the Scriptures that growth is to be expected.

The biblical expectation of growth

One would expect the apostle Paul to have something to say on this matter, so we turn to him first. In his second letter to the church at Corinth we read quite clearly that it is Paul's expectation that their faith will grow. It is not just Paul's *hope* that their faith will grow, but something that should be a natural outcome. They have been born (again), so they will grow. He looks for such growth earnestly (2 Cor. 10:15). Because of their growth, there will be opportunity for further preaching of the gospel in regions beyond Corinth (2 Cor. 10:16)—the opportunity for further growth as the Good News is proclaimed to more people. Growth brings growth.

Unfortunately, we can fall into the way of thinking which sees Christian 'birth' as the ultimate Christian experience, and the fact that one is saved, born again, as what matters; it is considered the be-all and end-all of Christian experience. No consideration is given to what ought to happen next. Birth is indeed essential, but growth is too. The apostle Paul relates that at one point he was a child, and his behaviour then was consistent with childishness; but he grew up and became an adult, and his behaviour changed accordingly (1 Cor. 13:11). Paul is using this as an illustration for the Christian life and therefore of the growth expected among his readers. Indeed, it may be a backhanded way of stressing what ought to be happening in their lives.

In his letter to the church at Philippi Paul again expresses an expectation of progress. The people to whom he is writing have accepted Christ; God has begun a good work in them; and Paul offers the assurance that what God has begun, He will also complete (Phil. 1:6). There is an ongoing work, a progression, a growth in their relationship with God. Therefore birth alone is not sufficient. No, God wants to continue working in us, moulding us, seeing us grow into maturity until the Day of Christ. Discipleship, sanctification and service are an integral part of Christian life.

Writing to the Colossians Paul tells them that Epaphras, who is one of them (Col. 4:12), is praying for them. Indeed, to express the full force of Epaphras's concern for his brothers in Christ at home, Paul relates that

Epaphras is constantly at prayer—'always'—and that it is earnest prayer: he is 'wrestling in prayer' (4:12). And what is he praying for? That they 'may stand firm in all the will of God, mature and fully assured'. Epaphras's desire for his home church was that they would grow into mature, adult Christians. Not stagnant and static, but growing up into maturity.

James makes the same plea to his readers: that they will reach maturity. He is making his point in the context of suffering. He encourages his readers to face their trials in pure joy, in the knowledge that the testing of their faith will develop perseverance (James 1:2–3). It is through their perseverance that they will attain maturity, or, as James puts it: 'Perseverance must finish its work so that you may be mature and complete, not lacking anything' (1:4). Maturity and completeness are exhorted.

For our final two pleas for maturity we turn to the writings of Peter. Peter resorts to the analogy of human birth and subsequent growth to illustrate his point. At the end of the first chapter of his first letter, Peter reminds his readers that they have been born again. Here he is speaking in spiritual terms, reminding them that the 'living and enduring word of God' (1 Peter 1:23) has been instrumental in bringing about this regeneration. Then, as he encourages his readers regarding their need to grow, he reminds them that the important agent in this maturing process is that same Word of God. Just as newborn babies desire milk which they require for their survival and growth, so Christians must 'crave pure spiritual milk, so that by it [they] may grow up in [their] salvation' (1 Peter 2:2). Following their spiritual birth Peter expects these Christians, scattered in various regions of Asia Minor (1:1), to grow.

The importance of growth in Peter's mind is emphasized by his closing words of his second letter. One's last words, one's last will and testament, so to speak, should presumably be the most important advice that one can offer, or long to offer. Peter's final words are a plea for growth: 'grow in the grace and knowledge of our Lord and Saviour Jesus Christ' (2 Peter 3:18).

So growth is expected of believers. Yet truly it is not something we can achieve by our own efforts. No; to quote Paul, it is God working in us who brings the growth: 'he who began a good work in you will carry it on to completion until the day of Christ Jesus' (Phil. 1:6). Anyone who is born again is expected to grow because of the indwelling presence of God.

Biblical condemnation of lack of growth

The other side of the coin with regard to the expectation of growth is the condemnation of immaturity. Yes, there should be growth, but on occasions the Holy Spirit is resisted (Acts 7:51), grieved (Eph. 4:30) or quenched (1 Thes. 5:19), no doubt restricting growth. In the New Testament we find examples of immaturity and its condemnation. We looked at the following two situations in the chapter 'A Well-Fed Church'.

Writing to the church at Corinth, Paul accuses some of his readers—or was it all of them?—of being mere infants (1 Cor. 3:1). Using the human analogy again he says that when they were young Christians he had quite rightly fed them on milk—Christian basics, no doubt. But, he implies, much as he would wish to change their diet to more solid food, this was not possible as they were still infantile (3:2). This condition was visible, revealed in their attitudes. Paul describes their behaviour as worldly (3:3), because of the jealousy and quarrelling in their relations with one another. They were also factious, sectarian, and their disagreements were based on which personality they preferred and followed (3:4). All this was a revelation of their immaturity (infancy in the faith) and also a hindrance to their being fed solid food to enable their growth. Although Paul pens no words of condemnation of their immaturity, he clearly implies that it is unacceptable.

The writer of the letter to the Hebrews takes up this same theme, classifying his readers as infants. They are still at the 'milk stage', they have not been weaned, and consequently they are unable to digest solid food (Heb. 5:12). They are still at the elementary stage—or perhaps worse than that—needing to be instructed again in the fundamental truths of God. We discover that those who are being referred to are slow learners and because of their inability to consume solid food they are not yet acquainted with the teaching about righteousness (5:13). To put it rather crudely, these Christians were still at the 'saved stage'. They did not have discernment with regard to growth in righteousness and holiness; neither were they yet ready for service (5:14). Sadly, we read that they needed someone to teach them the elementary truths of God's Word all over again, whereas by now they themselves ought to have been teachers. The writer was obviously disappointed that they were still at this immature stage, but was determined that they should grow up to reach maturity (5:11–6:1). So we see in these two letters that immaturity should not be the norm, and adulthood, growth in the Lord, is expected.

How do we grow?

Given that maturity, growth, is expected, and its lack is condemned, what is its source? As we are aware, we cannot influence our physical growth, and the same applies in the spiritual realm too. God does this work. After Paul has expressed his regret that the Corinthian Christians are still as infants, he tells them of their foolishness in trusting human agencies: 'What, after all, is Apollos? And what is Paul? Only servants' (1 Cor. 3:5). They are merely human agents. Paul may have planted the seed, and Apollos may have watered it, 'but God made it grow' (3:6). Yes, Paul and Apollos are human instruments, but they are as nothing in comparison with God 'who makes things grow' (3:7).

In a different argument Paul says the same in his letter to the Colossians: '[the body of Christ, the church] grows as God causes it to grow' (Col. 2:19). Paul is advising his readers to beware false prophets (although the term 'false prophets' does not appear in the text, I use it to describe some opponents of the gospel). 'See to it that no-one takes you captive through hollow and deceptive philosophy' (2:8); 'do not let anyone judge you by what you eat and drink' (2:16); 'Do not let anyone who delights in false humility and the worship of angels disqualify you for the prize' (2:18). From these statements it is obvious that opponents were trying to influence the Christians at Colossae with certain false teachings which Paul was seeking to counteract, even referring to such people as 'unspiritual' (2:18). Such a person has 'lost connection with the Head,' he writes, 'from whom the whole body ... grows as God causes it to grow' (2:19). And in his letter to the church at Ephesus Paul reminds his readers that it is in Christ that the 'whole body ... grows and builds itself up in love' (Eph. 4:16).

The 'means of grace'

In an old prayer for thanksgiving, one of the expressions of gratitude is for 'the means of grace'. This term was generally assumed to mean those earthly activities which enabled growth in faith. It is necessary to consider this aspect of growth. Yes, it is God who gives the growth; but just as a plant may grow thanks to God, it also needs some nurture and care from the gardener. The ground has to be prepared, the seed planted, watered and fed, and it needs to receive sunlight; without such husbandry the plant may prove fruitless, or at least produce poor-quality returns. The same can be said of our physical bodies. They grow, and although it is true that this is part of natural life, we can certainly help or hinder our physical well-being. Our bodies need care. A proper diet and exercise are needed to enable and encourage healthy growth. Illness may invade our bodies uninvited, but a healthy lifestyle generally leads to a healthy body, while an unhealthy lifestyle has the opposite effect.

In the same way, faith too needs some nurture and care for it to grow, blossom and bear fruit. It needs the 'means of grace'. Yet what are these 'means of grace'? In my youth, when the above-mentioned prayer was in regular use, I was taught that the 'means of grace' were what many would call normal Christian behaviour: prayer, reading the Scriptures, worship and fellowship.

These four 'means of grace' were brought together at the birth of Christianity. Shortly after the Day of Pentecost we read that the early Christians in Jerusalem 'devoted themselves' to the apostles' teaching, prayer, worship at the Lord's Supper and the fellowship (Acts 2:42). Nowhere is it suggested in the passage that these early Christians were told to pray, worship, and so on, and that this would be a precursor to growth. The indwelling Spirit planted a desire in their hearts to be involved in such godly activity. This desire was forceful enough, as those early Christians 'devoted themselves' to these practices, these means of grace. We can assume that they experienced spiritual growth in their own lives, in their relationship with God, individually and corporately, and in their relationships with one another. Also, there was growth in numbers: 'the Lord added to their number daily those who were being saved' (2:47). In this passage the four 'means of grace' were being exercised, not as a result of teaching, but as a consequence of their faith—a faith flowing from an earnest desire to know God.

We noted earlier the teaching of Peter on this subject, but you will recall that his emphasis was on but one of these religious practices: the study of God's Word. He said that adherence to this discipline would lead to growth: 'Like newborn babies, crave pure spiritual milk, so that by it you may grow up in your salvation' (1 Peter 2:2). Growth is an outcome of serious, sincere study of God's Word.

Similarly, towards the end of his letter to the Christians at Ephesus, Paul reminds them of the need for protection 'against the powers of this dark world and against the spiritual forces of evil in the heavenly realms' (Eph. 6:12), and although most of the items of armour he recommends are defensive, one is a weapon to be wielded: a sword. It is 'the sword of the Spirit', which is 'the word of God' (6:17b). Thus he indicates that when the Word of God is properly studied and applied the Holy Spirit is at work, not only in repelling the enemy, but also in cleansing and healing the heart, bringing growth. After all, 'the word of God is living and active. Sharper than any double-edged sword, it penetrates even to dividing soul and spirit, joints and marrow; it judges the thoughts and attitudes of the heart' (4:12). If the cutting edge of the Word is properly applied, growth will ensue.

The other 'means of grace' appear within straightforward exhortations and appeals. When the apostle Paul writes to the church at Thessalonica he exhorts his readers to 'pray continually' (1 Thes. 5:17), just as Jesus Himself had encouraged the disciples to 'always pray and not give up' (Luke 18:1), but in neither instance is there any mention of consequent growth. With regard to worship and fellowship the writer to the Hebrews urges his readers not to forsake the habit of meeting together, as some have got into the habit of doing (Heb. 10:25); while Paul, writing to the church at Colossae, expresses the expectation that they will meet together for worship and fellowship: 'Let the word of Christ dwell in you richly as you teach and admonish one another with all wisdom, and as you sing psalms, hymns and spiritual songs with gratitude in your hearts to God' (Col. 3:16). Again, no connection with growth is mentioned.

God gives the growth, then! Yet we must ensure, as far as is humanly possible, that the spiritual soil of our lives is prepared for the germination and growth of the seed of the Word of God. With this matter of growth we are dealing with something which is so basic as to sound trite. For what has been said regarding the exercise of the means of grace? In simple terms, we must pray, read the Bible regularly, worship and meet together for fellowship. We will need to add to these injunctions, I am sure, true regret for failure and an accompanying repentance. And such penitence must be in an attitude of truth and sincerity, as it is all too possible to carry out these spiritual exercises out of ritual and habit (though sometimes, in periods of apathy and dryness, it is habit which helps us to maintain our commitment to worship).

Surely now it is time to press on to the church in Antioch to see there the evidence and signs of growth which we have already noted. We have observed that the church at Antioch is a praying church, a worshipping church, a well-taught church and a unified church—that is, it is a church that displays the very aspects of a growing church we noted when looking at the means of grace. Even those outside the church had recognized something, perhaps inexplicable to them, but understood by us to be a commitment and growth in Christian standing. No doubt the non-Christians were sneering when they called the members of the church 'Christians' (Acts 11:26), but we see it as a compliment—a sign that they were true believers, disciples of Jesus, growing, maturing, not wavering. We are all aware of how critical those outside the church can be at times, looking carefully for any signs of hypocrisy or insincerity, or for any reason to make accusations of cant; but in the case of this church, all they could do was contemptuously call them 'Christians'.

So we pass on through the streets of Antioch to visit this church which is growing into spiritual maturity. It may be growing in numbers, too, but of greater importance is the fact that the individual Christians who make up that fellowship are growing 'in the grace and knowledge of our Lord and Saviour Jesus Christ' (2 Peter 3:18). And what will be the signs of this spiritual maturity? When among them we experience compassion, kindness, humility, gentleness and patience, forbearance, forgiveness and, above all, love (Col. 3:12–14)—true Christian character.

To think about

» Reflect on the 'means of grace' as a method of encouraging and enabling spiritual growth. How can you develop these means in your own life? Are there other things which we would find helpful for our growth?

» Gardening has been referred to as a metaphor for spiritual growth. Can you think of any other analogies which may be helpful in this regard?
» How would you answer anyone who implied that they were satisfied with being 'saved', or who questioned the concept of growth in Christ?

Chapter 11

An encouraging church

News of this reached the ears of the church at Jerusalem, and they sent Barnabas to Antioch. When he arrived and saw the evidence of the grace of God, he was glad and encouraged them all to remain true to the Lord with all their hearts. (Acts 11:22–23)

One of the simple longings of most people—and Christians are no exception—is to know encouragement. There may be some who seem to be self-sufficient and independent, able to persevere without any form of outward reassurance, but there are many who, in times of doubt or despair, yearn to know affirmation and support. There may be times when we experience a deep yearning for some act or word which will encourage our aching heart—but encouragement does not always come during those times. Oh, how we may long that it would!

Often encouragement reveals itself unexpectedly. On such occasions it has to be grasped eagerly and appreciated wholeheartedly. There are also instances when prayers of desperation are heard in heaven (and on earth!) and unexpectedly a servant of the Lord brings encouragement and grace to the supplicant. Encouragement often comes when we are carrying on with our daily living. Someone may say a kindly word or perform a kindly deed; or it may come through the observation of something that has happened elsewhere. We may hear of a generous or caring deed being performed by an individual Christian or by a fellowship of believers, and we are encouraged: our hearts are warmed and we are cheered to continue our Christian journey.

Encouragement may seem a small thing, but it is a very practical and very necessary thing. It is a noble Christian trait, maybe even a spiritual gift, to be able to encourage others (I say 'spiritual gift' because the Greek word for encouragement is derived from the same root word as the word for the Holy Spirit: *parakletos*).

Encouragement in Antioch

We turn our minds back to Antioch, which we find is an encouraging church. As with our two previous subjects, hospitality and maturity, we could say that this matter of encouragement is not glaringly obvious, yet it is there. When the gospel reached Antioch, many believed the message and turned to the Lord. There was a new departure in the preaching, beginning here in Antioch, in that the message was being proclaimed to Greeks (Gentiles) as well as Jews (Acts 11:19–21). And these Greeks were among the many who turned to the Lord. This was good news, but when the news of this revival reached the ears of the church leaders in Jerusalem there was evidently some concern as to the genuineness of this outbreak of faith. So to ascertain the credibility of this new church Barnabas was sent to check the situation (11:23).

I wonder, did Barnabas approach the city of Antioch with some degree of trepidation? What kind of reception awaited him? Was the church going to be suspicious of this inquisitor from Jerusalem? Was Barnabas fearful as he approached this ground-breaking church (ground-breaking in that the fellowship may have been made up of more Greeks than Jews)? A Jew among Gentiles! At least there was one thing in his favour: some of the founding members of this church were his compatriots—Cypriots (4:36; 11:20). However, if Barnabas had any unease or anxiety in this respect, his fears were soon allayed. Whatever may have been his reception—and I am sure it was a warm one—he 'saw the evidence of the grace of God, [and] he was glad' (11:23). He was encouraged by this evidence of faith, and in response did what we suppose came naturally to Barnabas, the Son of Encouragement: he 'encouraged' them (11:23).

Evidence of the Christian faith in the church at Antioch was an encouragement to Barnabas, and he in turn encouraged the members of that assembly. In other words, encouragement is infectious and can be self-perpetuating. Encouragement breeds encouragement, and Barnabas, with his reputation of encouragement, was truly the God-ordained gift for this church in order that this ministry might grow. But this is not an isolated instance of encouragement, so let us look at some other examples of Bible characters being encouraged.

Encouragement leads to joy

Following his shipwreck and stay on the island of Malta on his way to be tried before Caesar, the apostle Paul and his party set off again for Rome and touched land at Puteoli (Acts 28:13). Now began the overland march to Rome. When the party reached the Forum of Appius and the Three Taverns, they found that some of the brothers in Rome, having heard of Paul's impending arrival, had come down to meet him. This gesture moved Paul deeply; we are told that when he saw these men he 'thanked God and was encouraged' (Acts 28:15).

Paul wrote his second letter to Corinth partly in response to the news which Titus had brought recently from that city (2 Cor. 7:6). It seems that Paul was writing during a period in Macedonia when he was experiencing difficulty. He writes of having no rest, of being harassed at every turn, of conflicts without and fears within (7:5). However, in the midst of these trials, Paul was comforted by the arrival of Titus (7:6). But it was not just the return of Titus himself which brought comfort to Paul, but also the news which he carried from Corinth. Titus had related to Paul how the church had given him comfort, and of how they had a longing, a deep sorrow and an ardent concern for Paul (7:7), and hearing this encouraged Paul. He writes, 'I am greatly encouraged; in all our troubles my joy knows no bounds' (7:4). His 'joy was greater than ever' (7:7). He later says how delighted he was to see how happy Titus was following his visit to Corinth (7:13). This illustrates the joy that encouragement can bring.

Encouragement is revealed here as being associated with and engendered by joy.

We see these two—encouragement and joy—linked again in Paul's letter to Philemon. In this short letter, in which Paul makes a plea for the restoration into Philemon's household of the runaway slave Onesimus, Paul has some words of commendation for Philemon. The church meets in the home of this man who has 'faith in the Lord Jesus' and 'love for all the saints' (Philem. 5). It is this love for all the saints which evokes in Paul 'great joy and encouragement' (v. 7). Paul adds that, through Philemon's ministry, the 'hearts of the saints' have been refreshed (v. 7), no doubt referring to those members of the church that met in Philemon's house, but possibly also meaning the wider Christian community as word spread (compare 1 Thes. 1:7–9). Again, the connection between encouragement and joy is emphasized.

The effects of discouragement

Having seen that one of the by-products of encouragement is joy, we also need to look at the reverse side of the coin and note the effects of a lack of encouragement and even from discouragement. For this we turn to two examples in the Old Testament.

Our first example is the people of Israel. The background of the situation will be familiar to you. After Moses' meeting with God and commissioning at the burning bush (Exod. 3:1–10) he went to visit Pharaoh to plead for the freedom of his compatriots: 'Let my people go' (3:10; 5:1). Initially, when Moses informed the elders of Israel of God's concern for His people, they were pleased and bowed down in worship to God (4:29–31), but this response was soon to change. When Moses did visit Pharaoh his reaction was not what he had expected. Indeed, Pharaoh decreed that from henceforth these 'lazy' Israelites (5:8, 17) would have to gather the straw for the brick-making themselves, yet still maintain their quotas. The foremen were beaten when their assignments were not reached (5:14, 16). It does not need an inspired imagination to guess what the reaction was to such treatment: disgust and rage with Moses (5:20–21). Poor Moses, rather than being disheartened and considering capitulation, returned to question the Lord (5:22–23). The Lord's answer came down to a simple, 'Tell the Israelites, I have said I am going to free my people and I will do so' (see 6:6). But, because 'of their discouragement and cruel bondage', the Israelites 'did not listen to Moses' (6:9). In other words, the discouragement left them incapable of hearing what Moses and, more importantly, what God wished to say. Encouragement brings joy, but discouragement engenders deafness, as well as a feeling of being dispirited. We need to understand this as we seek to share the gospel with others.

We now move from a group of people who were adversely affected by discouragement to an individual: Joshua. Joshua had been appointed to take over the leadership of the people of Israel following the death of Moses (Deut. 31:3). It was a daunting task. If having to take over the leadership from such an inspired leader as Moses was not difficult enough, the task which he was called to fulfil—leading the people into Canaan—was equally formidable. This is brought home to us when we see how he is repeatedly commanded to be courageous, and not to be terrified or afraid (Deut. 31:6–8; Josh. 1:9). Initially, in the verses in Deuteronomy, it was Moses who sought to reassure him. Moses urgently and sincerely urged his young successor to be strong and courageous, and to be encouraged. After Moses' death, as Joshua assumed his leadership role, the Lord Himself spoke to encourage His servant with the words recorded in the book of Joshua. These appeals for courage suggest that there is a link between discouragement and fear: 'Do not be afraid; do not be discouraged' (Deut. 31:8); 'Do not be terrified; do not be discouraged' (Josh. 1:9). Whether it is fear that causes discouragement, or discouragement that creates fear, the link is clearly evident, and demonstrates the need to be encouraged. Discouragement must be negated and overcome.

New Testament encouragement

One of Paul's letters has an emphasis on encouragement. As he pens his final instructions in his first letter to the Thessalonians, Paul twice urges the Christians there to 'encourage each other' (1 Thes. 4:18; 5:11). In the first instance he is writing to them in the context of the return of Christ. Because Jesus had not yet returned, and some of the Christians had died, there were fears among some with regard to their deceased loved ones' relationship with God. Had their loved ones missed out on the parousia, the Lord's return, and consequently the resurrection? Paul tells them not 'to grieve like the rest of men, who have no hope' (4:13) and assures them that those who have predeceased them will not miss out on the resurrection; indeed, he says, 'the dead in Christ will rise first' (4:16). Be encouraged! They should not only be encouraged themselves by these words, but 'encourage each other with these words' (4:18) so that encouragement might be an ongoing activity. Then, to those who were beginning to harbour doubts about Christ's return, because of the apparent delay in His appearing, Paul reminds them 'that the day of the Lord will come like a thief in the night' (5:1–2). The world may continue to live in the ways of darkness, but this is not the way of Christians, who are 'all sons of the light and sons of the day' (5:5). Those who belong to the darkness are appointed 'to suffer wrath', but those who have faith in the Lord Jesus Christ have been appointed to receive salvation through Him. Whether we are dead or still alive, says Paul, we will all live together with Him. 'Therefore encourage one another' (5: 11). Paul repeats this exhortation to give it added weight.

These are not the only examples of Paul seeking to encourage the church in Thessalonica. We also read that Paul had sent Timothy to that city with the express purpose 'to strengthen and encourage you in your faith' (1 Thes. 3:2). These young Christians had had to endure some suffering for their faith 'from [their] own countrymen' (2:14) and Paul, out of his concern, had consigned Timothy to encourage them. Again, towards the end of the epistle, and perhaps with that situation in mind, Paul appeals to the church to 'encourage the timid' (5:14). In his second letter to the church at Thessalonica we see that Paul is still concerned that the church be encouraged to endure in their faith. He acknowledges that true encouragement comes from God and Jesus. These Christians have been loved and given grace and hope by 'our Lord Jesus Christ himself and God our Father', and Paul's prayer is that the Christians at Thessalonica would be encouraged in this knowledge (2 Thes. 2:16–17).

For one final example we turn to the Epistle to the Hebrews. Here the writer is concerned because of what we must discern as a lack of commitment to worship. Some had ceased to gather together for worship, so the writer pleads with his readers not 'to give up meeting together, as some are in the habit of doing, but let us encourage one another' (Heb. 10:25). The implication is that meeting together to worship has an encouraging effect. Perhaps we wonder what effect our being present and sharing in praise and worship has on our fellow worshippers. Here in the letter to the Hebrews we are told that it should be encouragement.

Now we look at a few verses where we see that encouragement is expected. As Paul writes to the church at Colossae he says that he is persevering in his ministry for them, for the church at Laodicea, and even for those who have not met him personally. And the reason for this constant endeavour in his ministry is that they might be 'encouraged in heart' (Col. 2:1–2) and also 'united in love, so that they may have the full riches of complete understanding, in order that they may know the mystery of God, namely, Christ'. Paul expected, and it was the intention of all his labours, that those to whom he ministered and for whom he prayed would be encouraged.

Paul's great longing for the encouragement of the church in Colossae is found at the close of that letter. Paul relates that Tychicus, his messenger, will tell them all the news they need to know about him. He will bring them up to date (Col. 4:7). But, as well as being the postman bearing the news, his visit also has the purpose 'that he may encourage your hearts' (4:8). Almost the same thing is written by Paul about Tychicus at the end of Paul's epistle to Ephesus: again, he was sent by the apostle to relay news of Paul's situation, but ultimately it was so that the Ephesian believers might be encouraged (Eph. 6:21–22)—and, through that encouragement, be able to persevere in the faith, in spite of the hardships they had to endure, following the example of Paul. We are aware that Barnabas earned the sobriquet 'Son of Encouragement' within the Christian community (Acts 4:36), but possibly Tychicus must come in a close second to bear that pseudonym too!

We find further evidence that encouragement was an integral part of Paul's ministry when he wrote to Titus regarding the appointment of elders. First, Paul listed the personal qualities required in elders: 'blameless ... holy and disciplined' (Titus 1:6–8). Then, turning to the matter of faith and knowledge, he said they should 'hold firmly to the trustworthy message as it has been taught'. Know the gospel! Be able to communicate the gospel! And why? So that the elders can 'encourage others' (1:9). Just as Paul saw part of his ministry to be one of encouragement, so it was his expectation that the next generation of pastors continue with the same emphasis. This is a ministry which is a work, a gift, of the Holy Spirit, in whose grace alone it is exercised.

So the church at Antioch is a church that encourages. On his arrival there, Barnabas found a young but thriving church, a fellowship which was obedient to the Word, active, praying, witnessing, hospitable and generous—and he who had a reputation for bringing encouragement was himself encouraged. And he continued to encourage them.

To think about

» To what extent would you consider that being an encouragement is influenced by the other aspects we have examined in the preceding chapters?

» Do you know someone who needs encouragement? What can you do to encourage him or her?

The essential Spirit

As we draw near to the church at Antioch, we should know by now what to expect when we arrive. For our final reflection we turn to the relevance of the Holy Spirit to this church and its testimony. Although we have already assured ourselves that the church at Antioch is a Holy Spirit-based church (see Chapter 6), we must return to this subject because we ended our previous chapter with the reminder that encouragement is a gift of the Holy Spirit—and a gift which is endowed not just on a few select individuals, but on every Christian through the indwelling of the Spirit. Also, we are aware that to be effective for God in any way—to be able to live a life compatible with His will—the Holy Spirit is essential. But let us remind ourselves from the Word of God of this divine necessity. Jesus said, 'I tell you the truth, no one can enter the kingdom of God unless he is born of water and the Spirit' (John 3:5). Paul wrote, 'If anyone does not have the Spirit of Christ, he does not belong to Christ' (Rom. 8:9).

The importance of the Holy Spirit

We start with the baptism of Jesus, at which time 'the Holy Spirit descended on him in bodily form like a dove' (Luke 3:22; see also Mark 1:10; Matt. 3:16; John 1:32). The baptism of Jesus in the Holy Spirit was not the same as that of you or I, but, whatever the difference, this event shows us the importance of the Holy Spirit in the life and witness of Jesus. For Jesus, the Holy Spirit's presence was an essential part of His being and work. Also, the post-ascension work of Jesus involves not just interceding for the saints at the right hand of God (Rom. 8:34; Heb. 7:25), but also sending the Holy Spirit upon believers—the spiritual experience which John the Baptist describes as baptism with the Spirit (John 1:33;

Mark 1:8; Luke 3:16; Matt. 3:11). In John's Gospel, when Jesus is seeking to calm the disciples' fears with regard to His impending departure, He reassures them by saying that there is no need for any distress as He will send the Holy Spirit to be with them. Indeed, Jesus affirms, 'Unless I go away, the Counsellor will not come to you; but if I go, I will send him to you' (John 16:7). This clearly indicates how essential the Holy Spirit is. We must not forget that it is by the Holy Spirit's work that we come to faith in the first place (1 Cor. 6:11; 12:3; John 16:8–11), but following our conversion the ascended Jesus sends believers the Holy Spirit as a guarantee of their inheritance, a confirmation of the sincerity of their faith (Eph. 1:13–14, etc.), and also as the power necessary for the fulfilment of an effective ministry (1 Cor. 12:7; Acts 1:8).

It was the Holy Spirit who came upon the disciples to enable them to be engaged in fruitful ministry. Just prior to His ascension, Jesus advised His followers, those who had been His faithful companions throughout His earthly ministry, that they would shortly be baptized with the Holy Spirit (Acts 1:5) and would then be enabled to be effective witnesses through the Spirit's power (1:8). Ten days later, at Pentecost, the Spirit came upon them as they were praying together in the Upper Room, empowering them for witness (2:4).

That collective experience was of course unique, being the onset of the life of the people of God in Christ, but what applied to the many on that occasion applied also to individuals. Just as this group was baptized in the Spirit for witness, we discover subsequently that Paul (Saul) was similarly empowered for ministry. After his Damascus Road encounter with the risen Jesus, Paul, who had been blinded, waited at the house of Judas on Straight Street (Acts 9:11) for God's next move. God sent Ananias, a disciple living in Damascus, to visit Paul and lay hands on him for healing and to receive the fullness of the Holy Spirit (9:10–17)—the essential Holy Spirit, confirming faith and empowering for service.

When news filtered through to Jerusalem that through Philip's ministry 'Samaria had accepted the word of God' (Acts 8:14), Peter and John were sent to investigate the genuineness of this occurrence—just as, at a later date, Barnabas would be sent to Antioch on a similar mission. On discovering that the new converts in Samaria had not received the Holy Spirit at baptism, Peter and John prayed for them and laid hands on them so that they might receive the promised gift, which they did (8:15–17).

Some years later the apostle Paul faced a similar situation when he arrived at Ephesus (Acts 19:1–7). He found some disciples there, possibly the result of the ministry of Apollos (18:24), and he asked them, 'Did you receive the Holy Spirit when you believed?', to which the answer was in the negative (19:2). Paul's response was to baptize them in the name of the Lord Jesus (not that of John, 19:3–4) and to place his hands on them, whereupon 'the Holy Spirit came on them' (19:6). This is further confirmation of the indispensability of the Holy Spirit.

Warnings against rejecting the Spirit

We can also see the importance of the Holy Spirit through some negative verses—that is, verses which exhort us not to reject or despise the Spirit.

The crucial and perhaps definitive verses are those containing words uttered by Jesus when He was being accused by the Pharisees of casting out demons in the name of Beelzebub. Having refuted this insinuation, Jesus stated that 'every sin and blasphemy will be forgiven men, but the blasphemy against the Spirit will not be forgiven' (Matt. 12:31). He reiterated this, saying that anyone who says 'a word against the Son of Man [i.e. Himself] will be forgiven, but anyone who speaks against the Holy Spirit will not be forgiven' (12:32). This is truly one of the most challenging statements Jesus made, and although many continue to wrestle over and debate the matter, Jesus clearly states that a hardening of heart against the Holy Spirit will have disastrous consequences. Blasphemy against the Holy Spirit seems to include the deliberate labelling of good as evil (see Isa. 5:20) and the refusal to accept clear evidence of the working of God's Spirit in Jesus. Jesus emphasizes that this as an unpardonable offence, and where those words are recorded in Luke (Luke 12:10), they come just after He has said, 'do not be afraid of those who kill the body and after that can do no more. But I will show you whom you should fear: Fear him who, after the killing of the body, has power to throw you into hell' (12:4–5).

In his statement of defence during his trial (Acts 7:1–53), Stephen accused the high priest and other members of the Sanhedrin of resisting the Holy Spirit (7:51), and by implication warned of the danger of such resistance. This is surely a warning to us of the necessity of having a right relationship with the Holy Spirit, the underlying message being that in resisting the Holy Spirit we are resisting God.

When Paul wrote to the Christians at Ephesus, he said, 'do not grieve the Holy Spirit of God' (Eph. 4:30). Do not cause the Holy Spirit distress, pain or woe. How might we do such a thing? Well, the answer is probably found in the context. When Stephen used the word 'resist', as we saw above, he was referring to the denial of what the Holy Spirit was doing in the revelation of Jesus as the Son of God, the Messiah. In essence, he was accusing the members of the Sanhedrin of denying that Jesus is the Christ. They were refusing to heed the clear message the Holy Spirit was proclaiming, resisting Him and His testimony. In the context of Paul's words in Ephesians, he is dealing with living as children of God and the Christian lifestyle. Paul is recording aspects of the former behaviour of the Ephesians and condemning any form of immorality: 'deceitful desires' (4:22), 'falsehood' (4:25), 'stealing' (4:28), 'bitterness, rage and anger, brawling and slander, along with every form of malice' (4:31), 'sexual immorality … impurity … greed' (5:3). He also sets down some markers with regard to genuine Christian behaviour; for example, 'Be kind and compassionate to one another, forgiving each other, just as in Christ God forgave you' (4:32). It is in the midst of such teaching about

Christian living, the negatives and the positives, that Paul includes this injunction, 'do not grieve the Holy Spirit of God' (4:30), revealing that unwholesome, unholy, immoral living saddens and pains the Holy Spirit—'grieves' him. Paul reminds his readers that the Holy Spirit is their guarantee 'for the day of redemption' (4:30). He is essential not only for salvation and for service, but also for eternity.

In his first letter to the church at Thessalonica Paul exhorts them not to quench the Holy Spirit: 'Do not put out the Spirit's fire' (1 Thes. 5:19). The next verse reveals that the context of this statement is prophecy, the proclamation of a word from God at the direction of the Holy Spirit (5:20). The apostle encourages the testing of any such word (5:21) but is concerned that prophecy should not be discouraged, even if sometimes it has to be carefully weighed. It is important that a word given by the Spirit's leading is accepted and applied. So the fact that the Holy Spirit is essential for Christian living and ministry is emphasized by the negatives 'do not resist', 'do not grieve' and 'do not quench (put out)'.

Walking with the Spirit

On the positive side, the apostle Paul exhorts his readers in Ephesus to 'be filled with the Spirit' (Eph. 5:18). This infilling is an ongoing, continuous process; these words could be translated, 'Go on being filled with the Spirit.' The Holy Spirit is not someone on whom we call just to meet special needs and circumstances, though there are often occasions when we need His power and maybe His protection in a specific way; nevertheless, He cannot be summoned in this way unless He is already present and we are seeking to walk in step with Him every day, living by the Spirit (Gal. 5:16, 25). His daily presence is essential. In chapter 5 of the letter to the church in Galatia, Paul gives greater detail about the influence of the Holy Spirit for daily living. It is He who enables us to live lives of love, joy, peace, patience, kindness, goodness, faithfulness, humility and self-control (Gal. 5:22–23), to be holy as the Lord is holy

(Lev. 19:2). The attainment of these characteristics would be impossible without the indwelling Holy Spirit.

Although, when writing to the church at Colossae, Paul makes no mention of the Holy Spirit when giving them guidelines for holy living, his list is very similar to that in the letter to the Galatians:

> Therefore, as God's chosen people, holy and dearly loved, clothe yourselves with compassion, kindness, humility, gentleness and patience. Bear with each other and forgive whatever grievances you may have against one another. Forgive as the Lord forgave you. And over all these virtues put on love, which binds them all together in perfect unity. Let the peace of Christ rule in your hearts. (Col. 3:12–15)

Like the gifts of the Spirit, these fruit of the Holy Spirit are an important aspect of His work. But it is important to note that there can be no effective ministry for Christ, and no genuine fruits displayed, unless the Holy Spirit is at work within one's heart.

When writing to his young protégé Timothy, Paul clearly states why God gives us His Spirit, with particular emphasis on the living out of our Christian faith. 'Fan into flame the gift of God,' writes Paul, and 'do not be ashamed' (2 Tim. 1:6, 8); and sandwiched between these two exhortations he says, 'For God did not give us a spirit of timidity, but a spirit of power, of love and of self-discipline' (1:7). We are not to be timid, but neither ought we to be overbearing, because to live effective lives for God we are dependent upon His Spirit: for power—to be influential—and at the same time to be able to love others and exercise discipline. We are dependent on the Spirit not just for isolated incidents—not when we remember to turn on our piety; not when we consider we are in a situation where we consider we are representing God—but constantly as we live our daily lives. While we will never reach perfection this side of heaven, when we acknowledge our dependence on Him for all of life, He is there to enable us to live in a way that is consistent with our calling and belief.

The Spirit's teaching and guiding role

Before we close this chapter, we turn to hear what Jesus said with regard to the actions and guidance of the Holy Spirit. Earlier we noted Jesus' emphasis on the inevitability of the Spirit's advent and His convicting work (John 16:5–11), but we also need to consider Jesus' stress on the sustaining work of the Spirit. This includes the way our understanding of Jesus and the ways of God are enlightened by the Spirit. Perhaps this could be classified as the teaching and guiding role of the Holy Spirit.

It is the Gospel writer John who relates the words of Jesus on this subject. Jesus' emphasis is mainly on the Spirit's teaching role: 'the Holy Spirit ... will teach you all things and will remind you of everything I have said to you' (John 14:26). Luke also records Jesus' words on the teaching of the Holy Spirit: 'the Holy Spirit will teach you ... what you should say' (Luke 12:12). Here Jesus is telling His disciples that not only will the Holy Spirit enable them to recall all that He had told them, but He will also reveal to them some truths which they had not yet learned—truths which, during the days when Jesus was with them, when their understanding was still darkened, their minds were unable to comprehend. As Jesus said, 'the Spirit will take from what is mine and make it known to you' (John 16:15). Also, when in the future the disciples became bewildered and puzzled, seeking to understand the truth of the gospel and to be reassured of it, the Holy Spirit would be their guide: 'the Spirit of truth ... will guide you into all truth' (16:13). And Jesus said that it was the Holy Spirit who would testify about Jesus, but that the disciples would be called to testify too, almost implying that as they spoke for Jesus the Holy Spirit would give their words impact and force and cause them to be revelatory, demonstrating that it was the truth (15:26–27). The Holy Spirit is the one who teaches us so that we become true disciples of Jesus.

So as we observe the church at Antioch, and as we consider these Christians, we see that they live their lives in the power and love of the

Holy Spirit. All we have learnt about the fellowship of believers at Antioch is determined by the presence of the Holy Spirit in their midst.

To think about

- How might we grieve or resist the Holy Spirit in our daily lives? In our churches?
- How can you ensure that you walk in step with the Spirit every day?

Time-travelled

Despite the popularity in fiction and film of the idea of time-travel—as we see in the success of works such as *The Time Machine* by H. G. Wells, the long-running TV series *Dr Who*, the *Star Wars* film franchise or the *Back to the Future* series of films—nevertheless, for you and me, travelling back to the early church in Antioch is something we can do only in our imagination. Hopefully, our imaginations have been stimulated by what we have learnt as we have pondered the Scriptures that relate to the church there and as we have sought a deeper understanding of this fledgling church. This is possibly the first church to have had its activities recorded in the Bible, and it is one of only a few churches to be revealed in the Bible uncritically.

What we have studied indicates what it is possible for a church to be. While what may have been projected through these chapters is a perfect church, an idealistic fellowship, which it is impossible to attain here on earth, marred as we are by sin and disobedience, this should not discourage us from seeking to apply, where we are able, some of the principles we have observed. Perhaps, above all else, we should be seeking to be part of a praying, well-taught church. When the Word is proclaimed the Holy Spirit can wield His two-edged sword (Eph. 6:17; Heb. 4:12); and He can propel the incense of our prayers to the throne of grace only when we pray them (Rom. 8:26; Rev. 8:3).

This church at Antioch not only stands as an example of what a church should be, but also carries with it a sober, solemn warning. Perhaps we will never know the reason why, but the vibrant church we have glimpsed from our study of Acts no longer exists. The Eastern Orthodox Church now has a huge presence in the modern city of Antakya in Turkey, and that church retains a Patriarch of Antioch. However, this should not discourage us from seeking to apply what we have learnt during our studies.

In closing, we reiterate the areas of church life we have considered and prayerfully await God's grace to enable us to 'grow in the grace and knowledge of our Lord and Saviour Jesus Christ' within our Christian fellowships (2 Peter 3:18). Remember, the church at Antioch was led by godly leaders who faithfully taught the flock from the Word of God. From this firm and sure foundation we have been able to observe how the lives of the fellowship were influenced in a godly way. It was a praying church; an evangelistic church; a Holy-Spirit-based church; a united church; a giving church; a hospitable church; a maturing church; and an encouraging church. From the few words we find written in Acts about the church at Antioch, may we catch a glimpse of how a Christian church should be, and may the Holy Spirit grant us wisdom to apply this to our lives.

As a final encouragement and challenge, remember that it was at this church that the apostle Paul began his ministry, and probably it was here that he learnt practical Christianity, which he drew on to influence his future teaching and letter-writing.